"Mount Shoop's new book, *Toucha[...]* [...]poca-
lypse, will become a classic for ever[...] [...]ing to
frame collegiate sports in a way that offers tangible ideas and inspiration for
refashioning this billion dollar industry so that it insures student-athletes
are accepted, nurtured, and prepared for the championship we call life."

—Emmett Gill
Assistant Professor of Social Work, North Carolina State University, Raleigh, NC

"Throw out the playbook. This is not a conventional play—and certainly
not a conventional book about big-time sports and theology. Marcia has
written an incredibly thoughtful and insightful perspective for all of us rabid sports fans to consider. Reading this book will help all of us in examining our faith and how it plays out in our day-to-day devotion to big-time
sports in our society."

—Robert Orr
former North Carolina Supreme Court Justice, NC

"Mount Shoop combines her knowledge as a feminist theologian and ordained minister with her years of experience as a football coach's wife to
navigate the reader through a spiritual journey into the world of big time
sports. Shaped by her religiously informed feminist commitment to social
justice, Mount Shoop offers revelations on sports's potential for redemption
and what we as a society can do to create a more equitable world for athletes, coaches, fans, and communities. A must read for anyone concerned
with the sexism, racism, and institutional power and abuse that plagues big
time sports in the United States."

—Cheryl Cooky
Associate Professor of Women's, Gender, and Sexuality Studies, Purdue University,
West Lafayette, IN

TOUCHDOWNS FOR JESUS
and Other Signs of Apocalypse

TOUCHDOWNS FOR JESUS
and Other Signs of Apocalypse

Lifting the Veil on Big-Time Sports

MARCIA W. MOUNT SHOOP

Foreword by
DICK JAURON

Afterword by
JOHN SHOOP

CASCADE *Books* • Eugene, Oregon

TOUCHDOWNS FOR JESUS AND OTHER SIGNS OF APOCALYPSE
Lifting the Veil on Big-Time Sports

Cascade Books
An Imprint of Wipf and Stock Publishers
199 W. 8th Ave., Suite 3
Eugene, OR 97401

www.wipfandstock.com

ISBN 13: 978–1–62032–919–1

Cataloguing-in-Publication Data

Mount Shoop, Marcia W.

Touchdowns for Jesus and other signs of apocalypse : lifting the veil on big-time sports / Marcia W. Mount Shoop.

xvi + 116 p. ; 23 cm. Includes bibliographical references.

ISBN 13: 978–1–62032–919–1

1. Sports—Religious aspects—Christianity. 2. Sports—Moral and ethical aspects. I. Title.

GV706.42 .M37 2014

Manufactured in the U.S.A.   06/30/2014

Dedicated to

All of my coaches

and

The University of North Carolina football players (2007–2011)

These have been my best teachers about

what is most true about sports

I know your affliction and your poverty, even though you are rich.

—The Revelation of John 2:9

Contents

Foreword

Marcia Mount Shoop in *Touchdowns for Jesus and Other Signs of Apocalypse* has crafted a thought-provoking, truth-seeking, and revealing journey into the world of big-time sports in America. The abuse of power, unfair and unequal application of rules and regulations, and the lack of protection and guidance for our young and vulnerable athletes are at the heart of this work. It is interesting and enlightening to be introduced to the working definition of apocalypse as used in her title. Apocalypse is not the end; it is the unveiling of the truth. Apocalypse reveals the things wrong with the world along with what good is possible and what is right.

Marcia is an extremely bright, perceptive, analytic, and passionate ordained minister in the Presbyterian Church, with a PhD in Religious Studies from Emory University. She has a keen eye for detail, is a tenacious pursuer of the truth, and has an abiding open-armed and open-eyed Christian faith. These qualities combine to make this a relevant as well as a revealing book for anyone who loves sport, respects the power of differing opinions and perspectives, and wants to contribute to a better society with a more even playing field for all contestants.

Through a unique combination of skills—athletic, philosophical, theological, and academic to name just four—Marcia poses the tough questions concerning race, gender, athletics versus academics, power and its use and abuse, religion in sport, and inequality and sexism. These questions need to be understood and addressed by the powers that be at all levels of sports and by every administrator, coach, athlete, parent, and fan. Clearly the journey of acknowledging, addressing, and correcting the issues that arises from Marcia's search for truth will have a positive impact both inside and outside of sports. As Marcia points out, "Apocalypse tells us that we stand to lose more when we don't ask the difficult questions."

In page after page and with insight, research, and experience to back her up, Marcia frames the questions, gives the background, and stimulates the reader to ingest, to digest, and to analyze and decide what is right, what is wrong, where we stand, and what to do. Her research reveals to us what we know but seldom acknowledge: we don't see things as *they are*, we see things as *we are*. We are molded and socialized by our background and circumstances to accept certain views of things and to reject others. As Marcia makes clear, we need to constantly ask and honestly answer the tough questions of *ourselves*, and never proceed on assumptions. We must review and examine our beliefs, our rules and regulations, our words and our deeds to assure ourselves that we are acting in the best interest of *all* parties. We can never accept racism, sexism, or abuse of power whether intentional or unintentional, in any aspect of our lives. And we surely can never become lazy or blind when managing, directing, or overseeing any situation where there exists the potential for the abuse of power.

Big-time sport is a predominately masculine world and the strong voice of an accomplished woman offers a very welcomed perspective. There is a humanity that shines through her reasoning and seems to lead to self-evident truths that are not emphasized enough in the highly competitive and combative world of big-time sport. In the pages of this wonderful book Marcia leads me back to my mom, who had a profoundly simple yet beautiful philosophy. Make your small corner of the world a better place for *everyone*. Help those around you when they are in need of help. Be kind to people and firm in your willingness to do the right thing. Listen more than you speak but speak up when something is wrong or someone is wronged. Protect the weak. Give everyone the benefit of the doubt, and be accepting of their differences.

Marcia has cut to the core of many issues in big-time sport. This apocalypse, the unveiling of those issues—both the very clear ones and the "camouflaged" ones, gives us a chance to confront, to isolate, and to alter or eliminate any problems and to then move forward. We can retain, reshape, improve, and expand upon the massive appeal of big-time sports in America by constantly examining and reevaluating the rules and regulations and their intent and their application.

We need to do a better job of protecting our athletes from unscrupulous actors in and around our games. We certainly need to provide them with the tools both educationally and emotionally that will help them grow, thrive, and succeed in the world after sports. And we should provide a "community opportunity" where they are accepted, educated, supported, enlightened, and protected as they move on and through their sporting experiences and into their lives. We need to emphasize and insure that those in positions of power do not abuse that power for their own gain or to satisfy a personal agenda. And we need all who come into close contact with our athletes to dedicate themselves completely to coaching, teaching, advising, and directing them in a fair, informed, equitable, and demanding fashion. Marcia's life experience, her love of sport, her deep Christian faith, and her deep faith in her fellow human beings leads her firmly to believe that we can realize the full potential and beauty of competitive sports by treating every athlete with dignity and by offering every athlete exactly what he or she deserves: our respect, our consideration, our guidance, and our protection in all situations.

The purity and life-enhancing qualities of competitive sport are what attracts us to play. There is nowhere to hide on our playing fields. We aspire to be as good as we can be, to play hard and as fairly as we can play, and to accept the outcome and move on with our lives. There is a satisfaction and reward in preparing, sharing, competing, and accepting victory or defeat. There is commitment, loyalty, and love among teammates and competitors. All is well when the world of sport is running as it should run. But, as Marcia has so clearly illustrated in this unveiling, it is *not* running as it should run. This work exposes the injustice, the unscrupulous targeting and distorting, and the unfair attacks and devastating consequences that are visited upon unsuspecting and unprotected athletes.

Read on and step up. Let's do what we can to make this world of big-time sports more reflective of the great beauty and grace in our games and less about greed, control, power, and abuse.

—Dick Jauron
Swampscott, Massachusetts
February 2014

Preface

I have given birth to two children. One came early; one came late. I have now given birth to two books, and while they each gestated with fits and starts for an excruciating amount of time, they seemed to have both finally emerged at just the right time. This book, originally conceived as a theology of sport, has shape-shifted a few times during the last couple of years. And I am thankful that it didn't "come early" now that it has actually arrived. While this book is still very much a theological project, it is more apocalypse, less apologetics than it would have been in its original conception.

For several years my husband, John, a longtime football coach, and I have done speaking engagements together on sports and religion. We give thanks for all those opportunities, both in churches and at the Natchez Literary and Cinema Celebration, to share our experiences and ideas with such attentive and interested gatherings of people. In those talks people often encouraged me to write a book about sports and theology. The ideas and stories that we shared in those talks resonated with people, especially people of faith who love sports. In the earliest of those talks we looked at distortions and at redemption, but that was before the NCAA investigation happened at the University of North Carolina. Since our experience at UNC, we have done these talks two additional times. We noticed that people still connected, but in a different and more serious way. I began to realize that there was no way to write this book without really excavating some of the most difficult things we had learned in our life in big-time sports. And so, this book gestated a little longer.

At several junctures I have questioned the prudence of publishing this book. There are those out there who feel it may be harmful to John professionally. But at every turn, John has encouraged me to see this project through. Especially after my "Calling Audibles" blog series on big-time football, I realized that this book needed to be written, but that it would not be done without risks. I know something is God's call and not my own when that kind of conflict presents itself.

I pray that this book can find conversation partners among many who love sports, whether you agree with where the Spirit has led me or not. This book is not a facile exploration of big-time sports, but it is a project fueled by a profound love of sports and by an appreciation for the healing power of sports. The book has found the light of day because of love—love of God, love of sports, and love of all those people who are tangled up with this world of sports—including the people I love most in the world.

There are many people to acknowledge for their love and support along the way. My husband, John Mount Shoop, occupies a unique space in how this project has unfolded and, no doubt, in how it will unfold from here. This adventure that we are on together started because of sports, stays interesting because of sports, and pushes us to be better partners, parents, and citizens of the world because of sports. By the grace of God we found each other all those years ago in Oxford, England, both intense collegiate athletes. And by the grace of God we continue on this journey together, both committed to the transformative capacity that sports has in human life. Our two children, Sidney and Mary Elizabeth, are coming into their own as children of God and as athletes in their own right. Their grit and their delight in the sports they love inspires John and me. I have an exceeding amount of gratitude for my coaches, especially Coach E. G. Plummer and Coach Dick Burchett. They made me a better athlete, but most of all they made me a better person.

Through the experience at UNC, many new friends came into our lives. The players who John coached were, and many continue to be, a blessing to our family in more ways than we can count. And many of their families, too, are dear to us. Sharon Lee, the mother of Devon Ramsay who played fullback for John at UNC, especially stands out as someone who has enriched our lives. Through the investigation she was the picture of courage and truth at many turns. She has reflected back to us some profoundly important things about who we are in the world of sports in light of the things we learned at UNC. And Head Coach Butch Davis and Tammy Davis will always have our gratitude for bringing us to UNC and for all they have done for us since.

The people who came into our lives because of the NCAA investigation have taken up space in our conversation around big-time sports in ways that have enriched it beyond measure. Robert Orr, Emmett Gill, Joe

Nocera, Richard Southall, Deborah Strohman, and Jay Smith have become not just conversation partners, but friends. And I venture to say we would not know any of them if it hadn't been for the NCAA investigation. And there were people in Chapel Hill who were with us before the investigation, stood by us through it, and blessed us as we had to leave that community. My writing group, Beverly Rudolph, Lyn Hawks, Susan Steinberg, Laurie Maffly-Kipp, and Katie Ricks, and their families were a centering source of love and support. Our family in Chapel Hill including our godson, Chris Dixon, his wife, India, and their children; my sister, Mary Faith Mount-Cors, her husband, Tom, and our nieces, shared the roller coaster ride with us in ways that have changed us all. We will be forever grateful for the congregations of University Presbyterian Church and Chapel in the Pines Presbyterian Church for all the conversations, prayers, and learning we shared.

My gratitude extends back into so many spaces, places, and faces where God's fingerprints in sports have been undeniable. I am especially grateful for Coach Dick Jauron and the model he has provided for both John and me in this business. I am honored that he is willing to add his voice to this project. There are many, many more people through the years to whom we owe our gratitude. All of the opportunities, all of the heartbreak, all of the hard work, excitement, and disappointment are experiences we have had in communities of people: players, coaches, coaches' families, teammates, fans, congregations, neighbors, friends, and family. All of these communities have taught us, shaped us, challenged us, and encouraged us to grow. I am thankful for the ways that we are not "free agents" but enmeshed in crisscrossing webs of relationships that stretch far and wide because of sports. I pray that this book honors all of these connections—what they are, what they could have been, and what they can become.

1

Introduction

Exercising Demons/Practicing Redemption

PASTORS AND THEOLOGIANS GET asked lots of questions—questions like: why is there evil in the world, is there life after death, and what is the meaning of life?

I get asked all of those questions. But they are not the questions I am asked the most. The number one question I am asked as a pastor and theologian is, "Does your husband think the team is ready for the game this week?" This question is second only to, "What do football coaches do for all those hours in the office during football season?" A close third is, "I have a question for you." This statement is followed not by a question but by a comment about quarterback performance or a play suggestion that the "questioner" would like my husband, John, to consider calling in the next game.

I have been in ministry all over the country, and this tendency has not wavered. The team's readiness for the next big game often seems to be the most pressing question many folks have on their minds. These questions used to feel to me like a distraction from "real life" matters like death and suffering and the meaning of existence. But through the years I have come to see them as a sure pathway to a profoundly real place in human life.

I've come to see these questions about the team's readiness or a coach's life as questions about redemption. *At the heart of these questions is the yearning to believe that redemption is possible and true.* Can we let ourselves dream of a moment when we can feel joy and delight in things working the way we want them to work? Or do we need to brace ourselves for disappointment, frustration, or failure? In this way, these questions are an unveiling of our deepest desires—the desires we often hide or repress in our "real" lives.

Sports generate emotions that we do not often have permission to fully express in other facets of our lives. Excitement, disappointment, anger, joy, frustration, and delight are authorized as full-bodied experiences in sports. We can jump up and down, we can yell when people make us mad, we can scold people when they disappoint us, and we can lift them up when they give us joy and make everything work. For many, the world makes sense in the confines of a stadium in a way it does not anywhere else. Sports can be where people feel most alive, where they find their identity. Sports can be where things are as they should be, where we know who is on our side and who is not. Sports can tell us where we belong. They can help us explore fantasies, physical touching, and sensations that are otherwise taboo. These expressions and their intensity are versions of religious, even mystical experience.

This intensity and this comfort is a curiosity to many, even as it is an obsession for more. This strange hold that sports have on humanity can seem disconnected from faith. Sports are recreation, dis-

> *Theology searches for God's fingerprints in human life.*

traction, entertainment, or even guilty pleasures. Many people of faith want to say that God is worried about bigger problems in the world than who wins games; and thanking God for things like touchdowns is an affront to the suffering in the world. Still others find God in the wins, the losses, the touchdowns, and even in errant field goals.

In these ways and more sports can show us what is truest about us—and such a revelation of our nature, our distortion, and our promise is nothing short of apocalyptic.

As a theologian, this is where I cannot help but fix my gaze—behind the veil of human distortion, squinting and straining to catch a glimpse of something divine. Theology searches for God's fingerprints in human life, knowing that we can never satisfy this hunger we have for certainty, for answers to life's deepest questions.

Sports may seem trivial to some, but when taken in total they capture our imagination and elicit our deepest emotional outpourings much more than any religion does. Thanking Jesus for touchdowns as well as our deepest longing for our team to succeed are ripe for theological inquiry. Indeed these deeply complicated dynamics of human life in our American culture (and beyond) are apocalyptic—truth-bearing and truth-telling. But theology is not simply about finding answers. Theology is practicing ways to see the threads of redemption in life; theology is a redemptive practice.

As it stands in our contemporary context, sports and our deepest beliefs are not always integrated in a life-giving way. The connection between the divine and sport can seem to cluster as polar opposites—it's either touchdowns for Jesus or God has nothing to do with sports at all. And the question of where or whether God fits into sports rarely explores the meatier issues that are tangled up in this object of so much human energy—like gender, race, and fanaticism. Not only do sports offer a chance to explore divine power and our human condition, but they also hold a mirror up to us about our most tenacious and dangerous distortions.

This theological project is a search for the redemptive capacity of sports by way of naming its demons. Indeed when we particularly begin to excavate what is beneath the surface of the spectacle of big-time sports, we can see some of humanity's most robust demons exercising their power. Because sports offer such access to these distortions it also provides us with a chance to call them out and take a closer look. Sports give us a chance to not just blindly exercise these demons, but to exorcise them. *This exorcism's purpose is redemption. Unveiling, naming, and exorcising the demonic distortions that big-time sports embody creates an opportunity to practice new habits, new ways of engaging in the communities that sports help to form. And these new practices have the capacity to be life-enhancing, expansive, and even healing to the larger world.*

This unveiling may show us more about what is possible in our collective lives together. This exploration may help us to see divine activity in a new way. Is there a mirror held up to us from sports that can help us be who we were created to be in a way that truly elicits our better angels? This question presses on me as a theologian with pronounced intensity because of the unique situation in which I live. I am a theologian and an ordained Presbyterian minister and I am married to a professional football coach. I am also a former competitive athlete. My husband has been in coaching for most of the years of our relationship. He spent twelve seasons (the first twelve years of our marriage) coaching in the National Football League (NFL). He has been one of the youngest offensive coordinators ever to call a game in the NFL. He has also coached at a number of universities. Our family has moved from Tennessee, to North Carolina, to Chicago, to Tampa, to

Oakland, back to North Carolina again, and now to West Lafayette, Indiana, for this vocation of his. In the midst of these places we've called home I have been ordained to the ministry, completed a PhD in Religious Studies, and served different churches in various capacities. Our marriage seems peculiar to many people. And while our marriage makes sense to the two of us, we have yet to meet another theologian married to a football coach.

Honest public conversation about the relationship between sports and religion has not always felt possible for John and me. While we have always sought out this conversation and relationships with people who have beliefs that differ from our own, we have not always been a welcomed part of the religious conversation in the sports world. We have been excluded from some groups because of the "brand" of Christianity we apparently represent. Some in the football world have dismissed me because I embody an offensive kind of religious expression—a woman who speaks out and even has a leadership position in church. And when it comes to our decisions to look more closely at some of the most pressing issues of our time around big time sports, like compensation for players' play or the ethics of the NCAA, there are not many in the coaching guild who feel free to explore those questions publicly.

Opportunities for John and me to do several speaking engagements together on sports and theology created space for us to think through what we've learned so far in our lives in sports. At a few points, this book draws from those presentations, even as it goes more deeply into many of the questions John and I have explored in our life together. From our

> *Recognizing God's fingerprints in sports takes looking deeper than the surface even when what we find does not serve our interests.*

difficult conversations late at night about how a life in sports was hurting our family, to our deep ethical misgivings about the materialism, racism, and sexism that big-time sports embodies, to the joy we have felt together at winning big games or in other athletic accomplishments, to the life-giving friendships we have made through sports, the complicated dynamics of a life in big time sports are etched in how this theological project unfolds.

And with the NCAA football investigation at the University of North Carolina (UNC) our lives took another turn as well. That experience in particular deeply informs the work of this book and, in some cases, the different direction that it has taken from when the idea for writing it was first born. Our experience at UNC lifted the veil on tenacious layers of many of the issues I had already planned to explore in this book. The apocalypse, however, in some cases has meant seeing some things anew in ways that deeply grieve us. Indeed, in many ways, our experience at UNC has changed how we locate ourselves in the world of sports. What happened there makes this work all the more difficult to do and, at the same time, impossible not to do.

GAME PLAN

Recognizing God's fingerprints in sports means finding ways to sift through the smoke and mirrors that can distract us in the spectacle of big-time sports. Recognizing the divine fingerprints also means we need to be able to name distortions and idolatry when we see them. Good theology needs to be engaged with the actual situation—warts and all. We are exorcising the demons that are exercised in big time sports. *Exorcising these exercised demons sets the gaze on the distortions that are embodied in sports, namely in big-time revenue sports like football.* These distortions are not always apparent to the naked eye and often embody humanity's penchant toward seeing what we want to see. Gender, race, fanaticism, religion, and big-time sports on college campuses are the places where we find demons to name and exorcise/exercise them with an eye toward healing and redemptive possibilities.

In chapter 2, "Apocalypse Now," I introduce some theological terms that will help to make this book more than chalk talk, but also theological, or God-talk. This project is, at its core, theological because it seeks both rich and revelatory descriptions as well as glimpses of redemptive possibilities. To this theological end, the chapters that follow will not simply describe distortions but unveil what they have to teach us about ourselves with an eye toward creating more conducive conditions for redemption to take hold. In the end, this book is not about dismantling big-time sports, but about calling it to own its redemptive capacity. Redemption comes with the most potency by way of casting out the demons that have led to diminishing returns rather than life-giving possibilities. Sports have much to teach us about who we are and who we can be; and sports teach us these lessons in some of the hardest places for us to deal with the truth and the consequences of our distortions.

Chapter 3, "Encountering the Fan(tasm)," takes us to the stadium where we can gaze at the dynamics of spectacle and fan(atic)s. This chapter explores how the confines of the stadium clear space for an unfiltered expression of ourselves: our distortions and our deepest longings. Why do people care so deeply? And what do we learn about who we are and can be when the veil is lifted on fanaticism in sports?

Chapter 4, "Man Up," attends to how sports embody our assumptions, distortions, and constructions of gender. Masculinity, gender performance, sexism, and violence are fair play in this chapter. Equity is not a lofty enough goal for how sports can take up space in the performance of gender in our culture. "Manning up" creates more generous space for real people to occupy in sports.

Chapter 5, "White Lines," explores the ways issues of race tend to be navigated in sports and what we might be missing when we simply look for the iconography of racial integration. This chapter seeks apocalyptic wisdom about race and privilege and how sports embody the dynamics of whiteness in ways that can be hard to see, even invisible.

Chapter 6, "Higher Learning," explores the vexing question of how institutions of higher learning and big-time sport commingle. We examine the shadow side of this partnership including how money, power, race, and privilege are intimate partners in how education and sports function. This chapter lifts the veil on the false foes of academics and athletics that have framed our culture's debate around big-time sports on university campuses.

Chapter 7, "Touchdowns for Jesus," is an unfiltered encounter with how Christianity is on display in big-time sports. Touchdowns for Jesus surely strip bare theological assumptions. Is it possible for divine complexity and generosity to find more substantive expression in big-time sports? Perhaps progressive Christianity's lack of presence in big-time sports tell us more about touchdowns for Jesus than we expect.

Chapter 8, "Redemption Time," invites the reader to consider the power of sports to kindle in human life the best of who we can be as well as the truth of who we are. Can we find pathways toward healing the distortions that harm us, that trivialize human communities? Can the deep yearnings embodied in sport help to feed more life-giving modes of relationships and community building in American culture? This chapter focuses our gaze on particular aspects of sports in which their redemptive capacity shows itself.

This final chapter will provide what may be a startling shift away from understanding sport as a trivial pastime toward an orientation that honors its powerful healing potential. Far from an apologetics for the superlative hype that swirls around record breakers, sporting events, and the "heroes" of sport, this chapter points us toward the capacity of sport to keep us in contact with the promise of redemption itself. This contact with redemption is where sports and religion may find their most life-giving connection. Redemption may come in fragments and occupy far too little space in our everyday lives, but practicing how it feels to anticipate it, believing that it can be, and delighting in it when it happens makes sports more than just the games people play.

2

Apocalypse Now

Don't be afraid . . . Now write what you have seen, what is, and what is to take
place after this.

—The Revelation of John 1:17, 19

I F YOU READ SPORTS Illustrated, you know about their "Sign of the Apocalypse" feature in which they point to evidence in the sports world that
humanity has hit a new low and the end must be near. Ironically enough,
given this is a feature in the premier sports-centered magazine, these signs
are often touchstones of how the sports world is becoming too important:

- "The babycenter.com website offers a Sports Conflict Catcher to help
  prospective parents plan pregnancies so childbirth won't conflict with
  major sports events." March 22, 1999.

- "Thirty-five Kansas City football fans last week signed up for Chiefs
  Grief, a therapy session designed to help people get over the team's
  Jan. 7 playoff loss to the Indianapolis Colts." January 22, 1999.

Or these signs show us examples of how the world is going to pot because
sports has lost something it used to have that was praiseworthy, like sports-
manship, dignity, character, integrity, playing for the love of the game:

- "In response to scuffles between opposing players at several recent high school basketball games, the Marmonte League in Southern California has outlawed postgame handshakes." April 4, 1994.

- "The Yankees asked the city of New York for $370 million in bonds for their new stadium the same week they signed CC Sabathia to a $161 million contract." December 22, 2008.

- "Wooden Award—winning BYU senior Jimmer Fredette is said to have been asked by school officials to finish his degree online because his presence in classes had become too distracting." April 25, 2001.

- "To celebrate Al Davis' 75th birthday, the owner and a group of old-time Raiders, including tough guys Jim Otto and Willie Brown, attended a Celine Dion show." 2004

- "A pregnant Chicago woman agreed to advertise an online auction company on her belly during the Super Bowl in exchange for two free tickets." February 12, 2007.

The sports world may well be too important and even a ridiculous caricature of itself sometimes, but the true nature of apocalypse invites us into a much more life-giving exploration than what popular understandings of this word suggest. The word *apocalypse* tends to conjure up feelings of impending doom and the end of the world. When we hear "apocalypse" we see cataclysm, a disintegration of the world, final judgment, and death.

The theological meaning of the word, however, points us in a direction of instruction more than it does toward destruction. Apocalypse is not the end; it is an unveiling of the truth—the truth about the world as it is now. Apocalypse reveals the things wrong with the world along with what good is possible and what is right.

> *Looking for signs of apocalypse is a quest for truth—truth that can both convict and transform us.*

Looking for signs of apocalypse is a quest for truth—truth that can both convict and transform us. Apocalypse can be a chance to change our ways. Apocalypse can be a signpost for what God is really looking for from human beings. The truth-telling, truth-bearing quality of apocalypse may mean the end of something and the beginning of something else. The divine invitation to enter apocalypse creates tension and possibility, but all is not lost. Signs of the apocalypse can only be correctly read if we are ready to hear the truth.

Apocalypse literally means a lifting of the veil. Apocalypse means seeing the truth about who we are, and seeing the truth about the nature of redemption. In this book, we are lifting the veil and letting sports hold a mirror up to us. We are letting sports instruct us about our distortions and about our capacity for redemption.

Lifting the veil means looking head on at the unfiltered truth. One hard truth for me is that I am a feminist theologian married to a football coach who has coached at the highest levels of the sport. Some would say that a feminist theologian should not be tangled up with something as violent and misogynistic as football—at least that's the commentary I imagine some of my colleagues in theology have ticker-taping through their heads when they hear what pays my bills.

In fact, one of my professors in divinity school, a prominent feminist theologian, told me how disappointed she was that I was marrying a football coach when I told her John and I were engaged. She said, "I thought you were headed for great things. What a waste if your life is taken over by football."

At the time, her words cut deep. And I, in a defensive posture and blind with love, protested that I was not going to let football take over my life. Two decades into this strange life I lead as a theologian and a football coach's wife I write out of the pain of that accusation and out of the fact that football does loom quite large in my life. Football has moved us around the country and helped to place me in contexts for ministries I would have never engaged in otherwise. Football has supported our family and allowed me to write. Football has taken John away from home for too much of our married life even as it has helped us to create a life together that works for us. It has been a source of excitement, disappointment, friendship, betrayal, lies, insights, and in the final estimation, truth.

This truth-revealing quality of football may strike some as a disturbing claim. Big-time sports especially can seem to embody the worst kinds of distortions and meaninglessness—even the bible of sports fans, *Sports Illustrated,*

> *Apocalypse literally means lifting the veil, seeing the truth about who we are and about what redemption looks like.*

seems to suggest this with the spirit of its "signs of the apocalypse." The signs of the apocalypse in this book point us toward truths that do not just cut to the quick, but that also bring along some redeeming possibilities.

Becoming better acquainted with the redemptive possibilities in our lives, in the end, is how apocalypse can save us.

Far from being trivial and distracting, sports embody our deepest longings and desires and our most tenacious distortions. Two theological touchstones will help us in our apocalyptic exercise to see hard truths and to embrace the redemptive possibilities in sports: *divine dependence and demonic distortion.* These two touchstones will help frame our exploration of sports in ways that may help us see things differently. These touchstones can help us go beneath the surface and explore some of our well-worn habits of thinking and behaving.

Just because these terms are theological doesn't mean they have to be hard to understand. *In the descriptions below listen for something that rings true for you. Take note of anything about these two theological categories that makes sense to you or makes an impression on you.*

DIVINE DEPENDENCE

Human beings are not free agents—at least that's what the religions of the world tell us. Christianity, the tradition that has formed me, tells us that we are created, redeemed, and sustained by a uniquely powerful God—a God who intimately and actively knows us and loves us.

> *Divine Dependence:*
> - *God at the center*
> - *Knowing who and whose we are*
> - *Absolute dependence on God*
> - *The creation of wholeness, integrating, enhancing*

Contrary to many of the narratives of American culture that tell us we are independent individuals, the narrative of divine dependence tells us that human beings are a part of a web of connections that make us who we are. Far from being isolated entities, we are entangled creatures, interdependent and deeply connected to everything that is.

Part of our interdependence is our dependence on God. Friedrich Schleiermacher, a nineteenth-century German theologian, put it even more strongly: human beings are absolutely dependent on God. Schleiermacher's idea of Divine dependence can help us to lift the veil. Schleiermacher uses the German word *Gefühl*, which is something like our word "feeling," but it is not emotion. It is the core of human consciousness about who we are and how we were made. *Feeling is our God-consciousness, our feeling of absolute dependence on God.*

The more we are in tune and in sync with this feeling of absolute dependence on God, the more we flourish as human beings and the more we can intuit divine presence everywhere and in everything. The more our God-consciousness is blocked by our distortions and illusions, the more our lives and our possibilities are trivialized and diminished.

A truthful life has God at the center. This God-consciousness, this *Gefühl*, is as simple as knowing who and whose we are. When we live according to this truth about ourselves—that we know we are not free agents, but that we are created, redeemed, and sustained by a divine source of love—then we cooperate in the creation of wholeness and well-being for ourselves and for the world around us. Awareness of our Divine dependence is integrating, enhancing, redeeming, and transforming.

DEMONIC DISTORTION

Despite our created nature, despite our deep and abiding connection to God, we human beings still tend toward living a lie. We tell ourselves we are free agents, we live as if our actions do not impact all that is. In a world that tells us we are on our own, our tendency is to live according to that distortion and illusion. A German theologian from the twentieth century, Paul Tillich, can help lift the veil on this tendency we have to live a lie. For Tillich sin is turning away from that to which you belong. Sin is estrangement from the ground of our Being. Sin is consuming the universe into ourselves, making it all about us.

> *Demonic Distortion:*
> - *Making the finite infinite*
> - *Consuming the universe into ourselves*
> - *Creates a distorted, illusory perspective*
> - *Conceals*

Tillich uses words like *hubris, concupiscence,* and *unbelief* to describe our estrangement from God, from our source of life and Being. He defines concupiscence as, "the unlimited desire to draw the whole of reality into one's self."[1] Counter to the way this term is often sexualized, for Tillich concupiscence is not simply striving for sexual pleasure, it is a lust to bring the whole world into yourself. Sexual obsession is just one mark of this

---

1. Tillich, *Systematic Theology*, 2:52.

tendency to let this desire for everything to be about us distort the way we live and perceive reality.

Tillich's "unbelief" is not denial of God, not disobedience, not self-love, but "estrangement from God as the center of our being."[2] Sin gives birth to the demonic: a pattern, a tendency, a distortion that makes the finite into the infinite. The demonic creates a distorted way of understanding all of reality. *The demonic fools us in believing that what is limited is actually that which is unlimited.*

Tillich uses the fictional character of Faust to illustrate the demonic. Faust made a pact with the devil so he could know everything. Knowledge is not demonic, but the desire to know everything is. Our demonic distortions show themselves when we make something that is limited and finite into that which is everything, into that which is of ultimate importance. Sport unveils our tendency to distort and contort something that is good by making it in into the All-Good.

The demonic is not an evil force outside of us conspiring about how to take us down. The demonic is a tendency within all of us that feeds and infects the patterns and paradigms of our lives together. And the demonic can, in turn, help illusions and distortions to flourish and grow into full-blown institutions and clutches of power and influence.

Awareness of our divine dependence is integrating, enhancing, redeeming, and transforming. Unconscious assent to demonic distortions fractures, ruptures, trivializes, harms, and diminishes us all.

THE GAMES PEOPLE PLAY

Children play to sort out and create meaning and understanding in their lives. Their play is their work. Many people would say that as adults we no longer play at our lives, but live them directly in our work. We do, however,

> *Sports clear a space for practicing the art of meaning making in life, for performing our identities and the character of our communities.*

yearn for places where our identity and life's questions play out. In many ways, sports give adults a space for such play. Play can be life-giving in this way. Problems arise when we are unconscious of what is at stake for us. Harm arises when we mistaken the hold play has on for the core source of our vitality.

2. Ibid, 48.

Lifting the veil from the way sports function in our society reveals just how important they are, and just how potent a force they are. Our concepts of gender, race, success, morality, belonging, and even of divinity get played out in sports. How can we befriend these aspects of the games we play and develop a deeper understanding of both our distortions and our aspirations? Make no mistake, sports are more than just the games people play. They create meaning and understanding and they have the power to feed both our deepest distortions and our most profound longings for life well lived.

As we move forward into difficult questions around fanaticism, gender, race, higher education, and religion, it will help to hold onto an awareness of our theological framework. We are working in an apocalyptic mode—exploring the phenomenon of sports for what truth it unveils. And we are moving through this unveiling with an eye toward redemptive possibilities. This redemptive intention means that we frame our exploration with the theological categories of divine dependence and demonic distortion. These aspects of our framework remind us of who we were created to be and how our condition sometimes creates dangerous illusions around who we actually are. Far from heralding the end times, this apocalypse calls for a new beginning.

3

Encountering the Fan(tasm)

Phantasms . . . should . . . be freed from the dilemmas of truth and falsehood and of being and non-being . . . they must be allowed to conduct their dance, to act out their mime, as "extra-beings."[1]

Soldier Field, January 19, 2002, the Chicago Bears versus the Philadelphia Eagles in an NFC divisional playoff game:

A man in front of me is loudly discussing different ways that my husband (the Bears' offensive coordinator and quarterbacks coach) needed to die.

"John Shoop needs to rot in hell."

"John Shoop is an f-ing idiot, he's too stupid to rot in hell."

"Someone needs to shoot John Shoop and put us all out of our misery."

For three quarters I didn't say anything to him. I tried to ignore him. After all, he had no idea that John Shoop's wife was sitting behind him.

The Bears were hanging in the game, but it wasn't going great. It had been an amazing 13–3 regular season (John's first full season as the OC) to get us to this playoff game. We had had some miraculous comebacks (including back-to-back wins in which we came back from twenty-one-point deficits with less than two minutes left in the

1. Foucault, "Theatrum Philosophicum," 170.

game) so I was holding out hope. But as the game went on I felt things caving in around me. I heard more and more voices around me criticizing John and saying hostile things about him.

My mother, a Mississippi born steel magnolia, as my father likes to describe her, was sitting next to me. She is not one to be violent and really isn't even that much of a sports fan. The man's rant against John was starting to wear on even her. When she turned to me with her hands clenched in a choke-hold position and said, "I could snap his neck" in her Mississippi drawl, I knew things had crossed over into a very, very angry place.

The hostility in the stadium was viral—infecting everyone. There was a groundswell of anger that felt dangerous and unruly.

I finally decided to give the man, who was terribly drunk, the benefit of the doubt. I would extend him some generosity instead of anger. If he knew I, John Shoop's wife, was sitting behind him surely he would tone it down. If I could give him the gift of knowing that, then maybe we he could quiet down and we could get through the fourth quarter with some dignity. After all, we were on the same team.

"Excuse me," I said, tapping him on the shoulder. "I'm John Shoop's wife, so could you please tone it down just a little bit?"

This outing of myself completely backfired. Instead of toning it down, I had just doused his rage with gasoline—now he had proximity to someone who could actually get John Shoop all the messages he so desperately needed to get to him. "It's a free country," he said through a tongue fat with alcohol. "You tell him he's . . . "

I can't even remember the words that came out of his mouth from that point on.

Right as he was telling me all the things my husband needed to know about football, death, and ways out of the city of Chicago, our quarterback went down and I heard a Bears fan a few rows behind me cheer that the quarterback was hurt.

Hearing someone cheer about an injury made something snap in me. I stood up and screamed "Shut up" in the most long, drawn out way you can say it. I said it so loud my vocal cords were raw and bruised for days. You would think I could have come up with a better come back, but that's all I had: "SHUT UP!"

I stood there shaking and crying and looking around that place that seemed God-forsaken. One of the other coaches' wives came over to me and helped me sit down. A devoted Christian herself, she had developed her own way of explaining this life we lived. She stated it very simply.

"Marcia, we live in a fallen world."

FANS AND FALLENNESS

Fanatic: a person whose enthusiasm or zeal for something is extreme or beyond normal limits; a variant of *fanatical* (from Latin *fānāticus*, belonging to a temple, hence, inspired by a god, frenzied, from *fānum,* temple).

Phantasm: an illusory likeness of something; figment of imagination; an illusion or apparition.

The fact that humans are sinful is not something I question. But this explanation for what happened at Soldier Field that day felt unsatisfactory at the time. It remains an inadequate framework for me to understand the dynamics of sports fanaticism. Looking back, I wonder if the other coach's wife was suggesting that I was naïve, even misguided, in reacting against these rabid fans. Should I have known better than to lash out against such a brute fact of human existence? Should I accept this dynamic and try to ignore it?

That day at Soldier Field it felt like some deeper, more awful fissure had happened than a simple display of everyday sinfulness. I knew we lived in a fallen world, and I knew people were drunk. I knew this was supposed to be "just a game." The horrible realization was that the anger, that hostility, that violent kind of reaction against my fellow human beings was in me, too. I was so angry that I had forgotten my compassion, my kindness, my love, and my resolve to somehow not let all the ridiculous fanaticism penetrate me.

I wanted them to know what I knew—that John was a good person and he was doing a good job. That he was up against problems within an organization that was making things impossible for the coaches. And most of all, I wanted them to stop. We had been enduring, and would for the next two years, people threatening John in restaurants, making obscene gestures at him at traffic lights, and calling our house with threatening phone calls when the team didn't cover the point spread. I learned not to watch any local TV, not to listen to sports radio, and not to read the paper. The Internet was just starting to explode as a space for fans to emote and analyze and chastise, so I stayed away from that, too.

Even the Christian radio station had an announcer who I happened to hear demonize John one day on a show unrelated to sports. What was true and real didn't matter anymore. A distorted reality had taken hold and there was no way to correct it. John had become a figment of the collective imagination. This phantasm generated by fans and media bore little resemblance to him and to the actual situation. My reaction at the playoff game that day came from a desperate place. How could I get the truth out there? How could I make this hostility stop?

I decided then that if I was going to be a part of this stadium-induced spewing of human emotion there had to be a way I could take up space there that had integrity for me. I could not change the perceptions of others;

> *If we have eyes to see, sports fans embody deep truths about human life.*

I could not vacate this huge facet of my life either. I needed more clarity on what it was that fueled the passion for them, what it was that divorced this space from human decency, from decorum, from some good old-fashioned team loyalty even. Was it alcohol? Was it the weather in Chicago? Was it the economy? Or was it something deeper, more primal, or maybe something even more hopeful than any of these possibilities?

I have encountered this kind of fanaticism over and over again since and have found myself in different spaces at different times. It can still can hurt sometimes, but I have never been penetrated by it to that degree again. I try to see in these fans something about human life, something about who we are and what we really yearn for in life. Somehow the sports fan embodies deep truths about humanity, about who we are and who we wish we were. And somehow this truth-telling is dissonantly displayed in the midst of fragments of truth and falsity that compose the fan(atic) imagination.

OF FANS AND FIGMENTS

Fantasm (*a working definition*): A person who occupies an illusory space in his/her extreme enthusiasm for a sports team. A fantasm embodies subconscious desires, losses, fears, and aspirations in behavior framed as team affection, thus becoming a likeness of him/herself. This likeness displays and elicits primal emotion while directing these feelings toward an apparition of what he/she truly desires. A fantasm is a figment of redemptive desire.

While human sin is not unrelated to the behaviors on display at stadiums around the world, the apocalypse may provides us with more insight than the category of sin has to offer. Sin, or living a lie, telling ourselves that we are something we're not (like we are free agents, independent individuals, the center of the universe, and the maker of our own destinies), provides a familiar framework for us that certainly helps all the mayhem and meanness that can erupt in stadiums make sense. But, for me, chalking it all up to human fallenness only left me with a growing disdain and anger toward the human race. That didn't feel good to me. My life in God's mystery calls me over and over again to find spaces of generosity. But what could that space be in the face of fans who make it their pastime to insult, to judge, to threaten, to loath?

I am sure it is no coincidence that my own spiritual journey was deepening during our time in Chicago to include things like centering prayer, silence, breathing, and other embodied spiritual practice. I began to detach from the anger that I was experiencing and that was being kindled within me.[2] I came to realize, after we left Chicago, that John was a placeholder for fan(atic)s, an apparition, a figment of their imagination. It was not really my husband they hated (they had no way of actually knowing him enough to loath him like they did), but they were angry at whatever it was that was making things not go the way they wanted them to go. *They were angry at having to feel disappointed, frustrated, helpless, and hopeless. They were angry that no one was listening to them, that they didn't have a way to control the outcome, that life is not fair, and that things never seemed to be easy.*

These figments of fan imagination sometimes collect around particular roles that people play in big-time sports. Offensive coordinators, for instance, are notoriously the recipients of collective vitriol and condemnation—they are the ones who are supposed to make the right calls, to make things work, even to be seemingly all-knowing and all powerful in their ability to get everyone to do exactly what they are supposed to on every play. Offensive coordinators are supposed to be the eyes in the sky who know what's coming and what to do about it. Gerry Dulac of the *Pittsburgh Post-Gazette* describes it this way:

> Of all the jobs in the National Football League, none should carry a health warning or occupational disclaimer as much as offensive coordinator, the Mr. Yuk of coaching positions.
> "If you did something wrong in a game, they don't look at the 59 plays you did right," [Coach Dick] Hoak said. "They looked at the one play that went bad."

2. In my blog series on big-time football I wrote "Dear Haters: An Open Letter" that tracks some of this journey and attempts to express the generosity to which I aspire. See http://marciamountshoop.com/2011/11/30/calling-audibles-part-x-dear-haters-an -open-letter/.

> Offensive coordinator might be the most reviled position in professional sports. They are second-guessed more than a weatherman, and their play calls get more scrutiny than a campaign promise. Want to start a discussion and see a talk show break out? Just mention offensive coordinator.
>
> In stadiums routinely filled with 65,000 or more people, the offensive coordinator is the only coach who needs to understand that 64,000 of them think they can do the job better.[3]

Perhaps, underneath all of the collective anger and frustration is a deep sadness that there really is no one who can make things work when so much is on the line. Those who we look to for such potency and efficacy disappoint us again and again. *Like Job's exasperation with God in the face of his life falling apart, frustrated fans have had enough and they desperately want something to change.*

The offensiveness of offensive coordinators may come from a primal, ancient place where we are angry with the powers that be who let us down as a human race. And they must, as with the gods of Greek mythology, be doing it just to mess with us. We fear we are pawns in their cosmic game of chess. The Greek tragedy was built on such arbitrariness with no ultimate source of justice to bind up the wounds of loss and harm.[4] The Abrahamic faiths (Judaism, Christianity, and Islam) offer humanity some assurance of an ultimate justice, a kind of justice that somehow trumps all the randomness of human life, all the undeserved suffering, and all the examples of wicked people prospering.

The promise of the Abrahamic tradition is that the Transcendent Author of the Law, the One who knows and loves and covenants with the human race, can and will liberate us from the harshness of the world with an order and a justice that is good, right, true, and inviolable. And for Christians in particular, Jesus provides the embodied extension of this "everything-is-going-to-be-all-right" and "all-is-not-lost" God. Through the Holy One, redemption is alive and well and true—even to the point of defeating the space where we are the most helpless, the most afraid, the most hurt—death.

The rhythm of the human story and the Abrahamic answer shows us our need clearly. This need gives rise to the messages of other faith traditions like Buddhism, Hinduism, and indigenous systems of spiritual

3. Dulac, "Uneasy Lies the Head That Wears the Headset."

4. Farley, *Tragic Vision and Divine Compassion*, 28–29.

meaning. We suffer and we die and we struggle to understand our role and our power and lack of power in the scheme of things.

EXERCISING DEMONS

The stadium is a place where this meaning-making plays out and we perform our dilemma and our agency in the collective exercising of the demons that posses and afflict us: fear, anger, anxiety, and despair. This dynamic has been embedded in the dynamics of the stadium since the gladiatorial battles and public executions of the Roman Coliseum. The Coliseum was a place where these emotions and realities played out on a grand scale. Everyone, from gladiator to spectator to Emperor, had agency and was on display. And this space authorized the construction and reconstruction of identities not just for the gladiators, but also for the spectators and for Rome as a collective, as a nation.[5] All were viewing and being viewed.

Self and nation were crafted in the Coliseum in Rome. "[I]n the spectacles of empire, all participants, including the audience, were on stage. To attend the shows was to take a risk, and because viewing was dangerous, it held great potential for the fashioning and presentation of the self."[6] These constructions of the self were potent for several reasons. Everything was important from where one was seated in the arrangements of class and status to who sponsored the various gladiators. And the crafting and re-crafting of self was intimately tied to a clear delineation of the "other."

"To have such knowledge of a thing is to dominate it, to have authority over it."[7] Entrenched in Roman culture and the dynamic of the Coliseum were these ideas of the exotic, the strange other, the alien animal that needed

> *Fear, anger, and despair are some of the demons that afflict us.*

to be destroyed. The Coliseum enacted a space for those strange, exotic "others" to be controlled, to be stripped of any power they might have, to be slayed. Any threat was extinguished and the Roman capacity to capture and defeat the chaotic was reified right before everyone's eyes.

The Coliseum created a world that made sense. It was a world of struggle, of contestation, of rivalries. It was a world where the self could be constructed and reconstructed with new challenges and new viewings.

5. Frilingos, *Spectacles of Empire*, 14–38.

6. Ibid, 63.

7. Said, *Orientalism*, 32.

Like the ancient Romans, we contemporary Americans like these dynamics of self and world construction to be on display—and as spectators (read "fans") we are part of the ongoing creation of who we are and who "they" are. And this crafting of ourselves and our collective identities is a complicated dynamic.

"The Roman Empire was not maintained by raw strength alone."[8] There were "countless moments of interaction and negotiation in which the subjects of Rome . . . struggled to grasp for themselves the truth of their society and their place in it . . . spectacle was a particularly effective mode for the production of authoritative knowledge about other and self under the Roman Empire."[9] And this forging of identity in the Roman context was always in the service of reenacting the might of the state.[10] These reenactments helped to secure the authority of the state and reaffirm where one fit in the scheme of Roman dominance.

It is not a stretch to find parallels between the Roman Coliseum and the American stadium. We can think of easy examples of how the spectacle works in our own contexts. We are obsessed with viewing and reviewing and being viewed. In our time we also have technology to help define the landscape of the world within the confines of the stadium. We are viewed and viewing at all times both in real time and on jumbotrons that reiterate what bears repeating, like big hits and spectacular catches. We are able to control our own ingesting of the play with personal devices that give us instant stats and commentary via social media. *Various collectives within the larger whole simultaneously create shared meaning, viral outrage, and hero worship with little more than a hash tag needed to create a movement or a new commons.* Websites spring up in protest or in support. And the spectacle is seen from all angles with Instagram, streaming, and the almighty television.

We are heirs to a hybrid acculturation that includes Greek influences, colonial impulses, and the dynamics of empire.[11] Greek understandings of competition, for instance, focused on the development of virtue and skill. And British sport in the nineteenth century was focused on developing characteristics that served the empire, like group loyalty and playing by the

---

8. Frilingos, *Spectacles of Empire*, 11.

9. Ibid.

10. Gillespie, "Players and Spectators," 301.

11. Ibid, 302.

rules.[12] Sport was a way for British values to infiltrate other cultures with different values. This performance of virtue, for both Greek and British cultures, was another way to enforcing values and norms to and for others.

Athletic contests in the Greek context gave spectators a chance to "catch a glimpse of the divine as it shone forth from the best of the competitors."[13] While this impulse to want to "be there" when excellence bursts forth is certainly within us, it can be obscured with other aspects of the common "tastes" of American sports culture. While sports in America embody aspects of several cultural lineages, some would say that the heart of the matter when it comes to sports in this country is competition and entertainment.[14]

With our theological framework, however, we have the eyes to see something more at work in our passion about sports. Think about the way being in a stadium can make space for otherwise unauthorized embodied expression. People who are otherwise polite, polished, moderated adults can enter emotional abandon at the drop of a pass.[15] Therein lies some of the mystery and importance of why football (and other sports for that matter) is not just a game for many people. It feeds a place in us where we are hungry.

At football games we get to cheer for the people who make us happy at the top of our lungs. We can yell at those who make us mad. And we can scold those who don't do their jobs or who disappoint and frustrate us. At football games we can jump up and down, dance, sing, put our arms around total strangers, and feel connection and community with thousands of people. We know whose on our side and whose not—it's as simple as the jersey color on the field.

And we can take a good hard look at our shadows—life is dangerous, life is brutal, life is full of people who don't play fair, and the wicked sometimes prosper. Nowhere else in life (past the age of two or so) are we authorized to express these full-bodied emotions about and reactions to the way life is. We can't do it in our jobs, in our families, in our churches, in our politics—at least not without being labeled as deranged.

12. Ibid.

13. Ibid., 300.

14. Ibid., 309.

15. Some of what follows appears in my *Calling Audibles* blog series in the post "Fan-Wise." See http://marciamountshoop.com/2011/11/17/calling-audibles-part-iv-fan -wise/.

POWER PLAY

The apocalypse exposes more than cultural heritage. The unveiling of the fan(tasm) reveals the intricacy of power and how it is inscribed in and through these collective spaces of joy, outrage, distraction, and community. *Feeling powerless and groping for ways to enact our own agency in situations that matter to us are not sinful appetites, but human needs.* We all play out this hunger to have an impact on our world in unique ways. The stadium provides a collective space for human beings to be impact players. The fan(tasm) uses things like lucky socks worn to every game, vocalizations at players, coaches, and officials, or sending angry or adoring emails to play with the exercise of power.

Fantasy football provides a mechanism for this desire to use power effectively. The explosion of its popularity, sometimes even at the expense of longstanding team loyalties, has given many sports fans a way to feel more in control. Fantasy

> *The stadium provides a space for humanity to be impact players.*

football allows you to choose your own team, craft your own game day lineups, and maximize statistics into winning combinations even when your hometown team loses. A friend of ours in the coaching world, Charlie Coiner, is also in the midst of developing software for football fans (First-Down PlayBook) to be able to call plays in real time alongside what is happening on the field. *These fantastical spaces for the fan(tasm) to play with power provides a cyber-sports pseudo reality that allows fans to not simply emote about frustrations but actually enact their desire to try and make things work the way they should.*

We engage in these spaces of yearning and agency as profoundly complex, fluid, and ambiguous people, not as cookie cutter examples of human fallenness. Everything from our genetic make-up, to the cultures we inhabit, to our unique habits and preferences condition our entanglement with the world. These are the kinds of bodies that make their way into today's stadiums—complicated, interdependent, and ambiguous bodies.[16] We have bodies that hunger for connection and belonging, bodies that have habituated unconscious habits and unspoken needs, and bodies that respond and react to what's going on around us both predictably and idiosyncratically. These are the same bodies that get swept up into sports-induced frenzies.

---

16. Mount Shoop, *Let the Bones Dance.*

In other words, we are not simply pawns in a cosmic drama, or machines programmed to lust for the curious spectacle. We embody flesh and blood uniqueness. We present and perform and have the capacity to "play" at and with different figments of our imaginations. This capacity to play and perform clears the space for phantasm/fantasm to communicate some of what normally percolates beneath the surface in human life.

We are "fearfully and wonderfully made,"[17] all of us—from the Bears fan who was fixated on my husband, to the athletes who risk themselves for their team, to the fan painted from head to toe in her team's colors, to the people who are there for the social aspect and barely know who won or lost the game. These bodies, fearfully and wonderfully made bodies, are "invested" with meaning in the stadium.[18] In today's world, in a democratic and free society, cultural power is not inscribed in the body through repression (as in an Empire like Rome), but through the encouragement of mundane, everyday norms and collective habits.[19] And we are both recipients and artisans of this "normalized" formative power. This kind of agency and interdependence means that we are not just pawns in a cosmic drama or victims of an oppressive abuse of power. We commingle with the currents of power and can unconsciously assent to power streams that are subtle, even invisible to our contemporary mindsets. More than we realize, we have agency, we have power that gives us the capacity to change, to be transformed through practices and habits that help to shape us.

When I notice myself practicing my own aspirational art of being present but not attaching to toxic emotions like anger and cynicism that are around me on game days, I am practicing being the kind of person I aspire to be. Maybe that's why football has such a hold on so many—it's a place where we practice using our own power. Can we defeat the enemy? Are we strong enough to work through pain? Will we be ready when the big play comes our way? Will things work out the way we dream of? And can we persevere and maintain our identity when things don't?

Why do sports fans care so much if it is just a game? The passion in the relationships between fans and their teams can tell us a lot about ourselves—shadows and light, identities and imaginations, fears and aspirations. Encountering the fan(tasm) unveils more than just our fallenness.

17. Ps 139.

18. Michel Foucault uses the language of "invest" when it comes to the way meaning is inscribed in and on the body through sport. Rail and Harvey, "Body at Work."

19. Foucault suggests this difference; see ibid.

The fan(tasm) is a figment of redemptive desire. Maybe the fan(tasm) cares so much because it feels like life depends on it, or at least that feeling alive does. The distortion comes in our blindness to our own yearning, in our tendency to collapse the universe into what is right in front of us, into ourselves. When we are blind to our own desires divine dependence becomes distorted dependence on a finite reality that can never satisfy our appetite for redemption.

If we "free" the fantasm from the "dilemmas of truth and falsehood" and allow them to "conduct their dance, to act out their mime" then we see them as a mirror for who we are, not simply as another example of human depravity. That Bears fan at the playoff game (beer intake notwithstanding) was testifying to his desire to make an impact, to have the power to fashion a world where things work the way they should. My "reality check" to him did not interrupt his play, and why should it? The fan(tasm) can have the space to play with its phantastic figments when we allow it to expand its stage into the deepest longings of human existence. Truly humanizing that man would have looked very different than telling him who I was. I would have instead asked him to tell me who he was. Only then could I, too, begin to play with my own imagination, with my own power to believe that somewhere in the midst of his rant was a child of God hungry for a better world.

4

Man Up

A state university in 2011, mandatory football team meeting:

A preacher from an area non-denominational church, who was invited to speak to the whole team at a mandatory meeting about "toughness," begins his talk by flashing up a traditional picture of Jesus. He proceeds to tell the players, in a loud and aggressive voice, that this picture makes Jesus looks like a sissy, like a girl. "Jesus wasn't a sissy. He was a warrior," he said. The preacher told the players that they needed to "man up." "Whether you start a fight or not, you should finish it. Jesus knew how to finish fights and he was not a sissy." This preacher went on to explain to the football team that our culture has emasculated men and feminized Jesus. "Man up," he said, "don't let his happen to you." The preacher was there with his three young sons.

For many women, as they move in sport, a space surrounds us in imagination that we are not free to move beyond; the space available to our movement is constricted space.[1]

(EN)GENDER(ED) EXTREMITIES

THE WORLD OF FOOTBALL is hyper-masculine, to state an obvious description. My proximity to this male dominated space provides a sometimes bizarre foil to my experience and identity as a theologian, particularly

---

1. Young, "Throwing Like a Girl," 263.

as a theologian with feminist training and sensitivities. For many men who occupy the football world, the things theologians, especially feminist theologians, talk about are in an almost foreign language and, undoubtedly, in some instances deeply troubling. And in some of the feminist circles I occupy, many can barely imagine how the world of football actually operates. More than that, they wonder how I can operate in that world and maintain my integrity, or even sanity, as a woman.

These dissonant communities that I occupy do not settle into many harmonious spaces. They contradict and even condemn each other. They accuse and they dismiss each other. Sometimes they are even repulsed by each other. This chapter seeks to abide in those contested spaces in order to unveil the distortions around gender construction that sport reifies. A clear look at these extremities could also reveal some promising spaces ripe for more complexity to find expression. Like good theater, these extremes simultaneously display distortions, refractions, and life-giving invitations.

CONSTRAINED SPACES

I came along in a time when women's sports were starting to be normalized. Title IX was ratified just three years after I was born in the heart of Kentucky basketball country. Things were far from equitable for women in many ways. But, while my opportunities were limited, they were

> *Title IX was ratified in 1972 and requires gender equity for boys and girls in every educational program that receives federal funding.*

startling in their possibility from the perspectives of my mother and my grandmother. I ran cross-country and track on teams that won repeated state championships in Kentucky. We were nurtured and celebrated for our accomplishments even as we fought early on for something other than hand-me-down uniforms and spikes from boys' track teams of the past.

I had the honor of being in the first group of ten national finalists for the NCAA Woman of the Year award in 1991. Robin Roberts interviewed all of the finalists and we got to spend time with tennis great and pioneer, Althea Gibson. The trip for the national award ceremony was a powerful few days of awareness-raising for me. My mother had told me the stories about her playing basketball and only being able to dribble twice and play half court. I had seen the pictures of my grandmother wearing a dress to play basketball at Belhaven College. Even with these touchstones of where things had been for women in sports, the Woman of the Year experience created a new level of critical consciousness in me. I realized anew that my participation in sports was possible because of women who transgressed even as they conformed.

Althea Gibson told us about her love for competing and how hard it was to do because of the absolute absence of funding for women athletes. She was excited about the NCAA Woman of the Year award and the monetary support that it extended into women's athletics in colleges and universities. *It kindled the question in me of whether women are able to take up space in sports with feminine modes of being or by appropriating masculine ones.* That dichotomy seemed false to me then, and it continues to create a problematic dualism as I live out my adult life in the world of sports.

Now as a mother, I see my elementary school-aged daughter enjoy opportunities way beyond mine. She has access to multiple sports even at her young age. The quest for equity continues even as expectations and standards shift and change with generations. The questions linger about how to best encourage the kind of participation in sports across gender that is the most constructive for all athletes and for society. *Is it equity that we're after—that girls can do everything boys can do, or is it something else?* Are women authorized to occupy the world of sports as women in all our complexity or is this world one in which women must appropriate masculinized modalities to succeed? Is appropriating masculinity the preferred mode of comportment for women in a male-dominated culture?[2] These questions only get us to a still deeper and more profound question: *how much does the world of sport lean on gender extremities and dichotomies to function and even to flourish? And do these extremities create the conditions for the true flourishing of real human beings?*

FEMININITY AND FOOTBALL

It is the quest for access and equity that exorcises some of the gendered demons that sport embodies. Football stands at the extreme of this quest. The size of the teams, the expense of the sport, the revenue it generates for

2. Iris Marion Young's "Throwing like a Girl" and, even more directly, her essay "Throwing Like a Girl Revisited" pose these questions about the nature of the embodied mode that women seek to inhabit in masculinized spaces—if they are universal modes from which women are constrained or excluded or if they are specifically masculine modes that have been rendered universal in a patriarchal culture.

some universities (not all by any stretch), and its hyper-masculinity make it a hyperbolic example. Football occupies the extreme because it remains perhaps the only sport that has not undergone an influx of female players and coaches. While the number of female football fans has increased, women and girls do not have access to the actual play and power structures of football in any substantive way.

As far as women and football go, coaches' wives like me compose the female group who occupy any sort of close proximity to the everyday ins and outs of the football world. And we are not invited to occupy that space with any formal power. We have only threads of opportunity for the informal exercise of power in the ways decisions are made and power is wielded. Within that constrained space football coaches' wives are expected to conform to several norms if we want to survive in this world, even though we are a varied group of women with different experiences and competencies.

> *Do sports depend on gender stereotypes that prop up particular expressions of masculinity?*

Football coaches' wives are to enact a supportive role to our spouses—taking care of everything from childcare to lawn care to attending games and recruiting functions properly dressed. We are to accept things like our spouses' long work hours and seven-day work weeks, as well as frequent moves. And we are to do all of these things competently without much input from our spouses so that they can be at work unencumbered by the details of home. While John coached in the NFL there were teams he worked for where I could not even enter his office space because I was female and team policies barred women from those spaces. This male enclave encourages stark separations in gender roles. Men work and earn the income to support their families, and women take care of all the demands of life at home. Women are the behind-the-scenes support system for their husbands and oftentimes for the team as well.

Coaches' wives who do have careers have to find ways to make our lives work in the midst of all the transience and all of the childcare and home care that we oftentimes have to take care of alone. In some of the places we lived, when I attempted to work outside the home, the team of babysitters and family assistants we needed to prop up the necessities of life getting done was extreme and often untenable.

GENDER CONDITIONING: FLEXING MASCULINE MUSCLES

These complicated dynamics bring with them multiple questions and spaces for inquiry. These contested spaces create the tension needed for exorcising demons that distort our lived conditions as gendered beings. *"Manning Up" means unveiling the systemic distortions and chronic contortions of sports that continue to prop up exclusionary and even abusive models of masculinity.* These distortions are particularly compelling for us to consider because they are exercised at the expense of more than just robust constructions of femininity. These demonic distortions have their way also at the expense of vital space for men. These constrained spaces can make it difficult for real, complicated people of all genders to occupy them and to thrive.

How do sports communicate and perform our communal aspirations and standards around gender roles? How do sports contort gender? Can sports function without strict gender delineations? How much do the frameworks and mentalities of sports require the performance of gender stereotypes, and how much have these same stereotypes trivialized sport?

These are questions that invite us to unveil our distortions without fear. Our fears around questions of gender are often deep, often unconscious. And these fears rest on visceral assumptions that there is too much at stake for us to allow for difficult questions.

> *Letting fear lead the way often leads to enforced conformity.*

When fear leads the way, conformity is often the strategy for tamping it down. An apocalyptic gaze invites a courageous kind of trust. *Apocalypse tells us that what we stand to lose when we don't ask the difficult questions is actually the more radical threat to our humanity than the erosion of the social convention in question is.* We have more to lose if we don't exorcise the demon.

The essentials of being masculine and feminine in contemporary society are not as rigid as they once were. There are blurred lines where there use to be sharp distinctions. As gender performance in a culture becomes more malleable, there often is a counter-force of retrenchment of gender roles in male-dominated spaces. *As lines are blurred in the larger culture, spaces that have defined themselves through gender distinctions grasp for clarity of identity and for their distinctiveness to stay in place.* The exclusion of those who blur lines in those male-dominated spaces becomes even more important when gender malleability increases in the larger culture.

While raising a daughter brings with it its own particular kinds of concerns and anxieties for her as a developing athlete and as a young girl in such close proximity to the world of football, raising a son has brought with it an unexpected set of heartbreaking realities. Not the least of these realities is the realization that to find his way into manhood my son increasingly feels pulled toward developing competency in some activity that involves the performance of dominance, force, and toughness. While grit is a character trait we all need in order to survive the rigors of human life, the mandated performance of dominance and force is a more complicated and sometimes troubling rite of passage for boys. While I understand the value of knowing that one can defend and protect oneself, the equation of this kind of confidence with dominance is dangerous. The overlay of force is a particular aspect of this need to "finish a fight" where gender-cloaked distortions can take hold most tenaciously.

Witnessing the restrictive and constrictive spaces that men and boys have to occupy in sports, especially in a contact sport like football, makes these questions pressing from both sides. Manning up constricts and constrains us all. How to exorcise the demons, so that we might better exercise our vitality as human beings, is the question that surfaces in this apocalypse.

MUSCULAR CHRISTIANITY

> "I believe we're so passionate about football because it embodies everything we love about American exceptionalism. Merit is rewarded, not punished. Masculinity is celebrated, not feminized."
>
> —Talk radio host Steve Deace

We need to account for how sports have been employed to demonstrate and reify masculinity and masculine power. Historically, this employment of sports is no more clearly unveiled than in the "muscular Christianity" movement of the late nineteenth and twentieth centuries in America. While this movement has British origins, the American context easily adopted these values in the world of mainline Protestantism in the early 1900s. Muscular Christianity bares the anxiety that found a home in men and male-run institutions (like churches and universities) around the danger of the feminization of American and Christian cultures.

Fears around the feminization of Christianity helped to give birth to and nurture the YMCA (Young Men's Christian Association) movement led by "muscular Christians" in the mainline Protestant structures of American society. These same fears changed the ways churches were constructed. More and more churches decided to include gymnasia in their plans, and discipleship for men became tethered to toughness and the increase of male-only spaces like the Masons at the turn of the century. In order to stop the slippage of masculinity into feminized modes, these masculinized spaces were framed by the performance of particular expressions of masculinity, which included athleticism.[3] The Social Gospel movement helped to feed these anxieties.[4] The compassionate Jesus threatened the model of the rugged individual who conformed to the industrial, capitalistic norms of American society.

Narratives of self-made men, of men who were not soft, but who knew how to finish a fight, found a space for play and performance in the increasing popularity of sports like football. And the hyper-masculine character of this sport helped to secure its place in the hearts of Americans—it performs that which reflects back to us who we should be, who we need to be.[5] And it displays clear lines around gender so much so that spaces developed on the outskirts of the gridiron for the performance of femininity with equal clarity.

Cheerleaders appeared on the sidelines to embody the ideals of objectified femininity—there on display in the service of men's pleasure and reflecting hyper-masculinized constructions of women as petite, pretty, and supportive of the male activities that are the real center of attention. Ironically, for the first twenty-five years of the existence of cheerleaders, this activity, too, was restricted to only male participants. Cheerleading began as a cheering section of a few men at Princeton in the late 1800s. During World War II, women filled the gap of men gone to war in this cheerleading role. And today, 90 percent of cheerleaders are women.[6]

---

3. Putney, *Muscular Christianity*, 200.

4. The Social Gospel movement emerged in the late nineteenth and early twentieth centuries in North America as a reaction to the dehumanizing effects of Industrialization. While this movement was theologically diverse, it tended to revolve around calls to honor the humanity of workers with more just systems. It emphasized Jesus' ministries of justice and compassion as models for human society. These emphases created tension around the norms of Industrialization like individualism and unhindered capitalism.

5. This sentiment is clearly stated in the quote by Steve Deace (see text box above) and elaborated upon in his article "Don't Ruin the Game We Love."

6. See http://cheerunion.org/Content.aspx/History.

As American culture has moved through shifts and changes in gender roles and identities in the second half of the twentieth century, cheerleading has morphed to reflect different aspects of sports culture. On the one hand, there are some cheerleading programs that have become more and more focused on amazing gymnastic feats, so much so that 66 percent of all catastrophic injuries in girls' high school sports in the last twenty-five years have happened in cheerleading.[7] In 2013 the American Academy of Pediatrics recommended that cheerleading be designated as a sport in order to make safety measures and medical interventions more adequate and consistent. We are asking girls and young women to be athletic, even to the extreme in some cases, often without affording them the same status and protection that having cheerleading classified as a sport would give them.

On the other hand, cheerleaders at the highest levels of exposure in the world of sports have become increasingly sexualized and hyperfeminized. One need look no further than the "Cheerleader of the Week" feature in *Sports Illustrated* for evidence of how increasingly caricatured female bodies define the contours of femininity that surround the world of big-time sports.[8] At both these extremes, real female bodies are reflective of constraining caricatures and expectations for how women can make their mark on the outskirts of largely male dominated sporting events.

The anatomy of the football field creates a template for a settled framework around gender. This appearance and performance of gender is propped up by the participants, by the observers, and by the kinds of achievements and behaviors that are affirmed and handsomely rewarded in American culture. These frameworks around gender have also been propped up by theological and confessional scaffolding constructed into this system through the presence of religious organizations like Fellowship of Christian Athletes (FCA), Athletes in Action, and Campus Crusade for Christ.[9] These parachurch movements are children of the muscular Christianity movement; some even refer to them as "neo-muscular Christian

7. See http://www.cbsnews.com/news/pediatricians-want-cheerleading-called-a -sport-over-injury-risk/.

8. *Sports Illustrated*, "Cheerleader of the Week." See the following: http://sportsillus-trated.cnn.com/cheerleaders/photos/1307/cheerleader-of-the-week-madonna/; http://sportsillustrated.cnn.com/cheerleaders/photos/1311/cheerleader-of-the-week-chantel/; http://sportsillustrated.cnn.com/multimedia/photo_gallery/cheerleaders/.

9. More about the religious dynamics that these groups bring to big-time sports is explored in chapter 7, "Touchdowns for Jesus."

groups." These groups often serve as modern-day evangelists for the essential qualities of gender identities.[10]

Maintaining gender roles is, no doubt, not how groups like FCA consciously define their role in the sports world. The particular ways that Christianity is most often framed in their work, however, often includes a traditional view of how women are involved in church leadership.[11] On every team John has ever coached there has been team chaplain who was placed there by one of these organizations. Over dinner one night the chaplain on an NFL team John coached used biblical references to explain to John that I, his wife, was not being biblical by being in the ministry. On that same team, I was asked to leave the wives' Bible study when I suggested there might be other perspectives about marriage in addition to one that we were reading that asserted women are required to submit to and obey their husbands.

These constricted spaces embody both aspirations and distortions, both reflections of reality and illusions of patriarchal rhetoric. The constraints, however, are not without a cost even for those who occupy the top of the gender hierarchy in these hyper-masculine spaces. Psychological theories point us toward the cost that comes in men's lives the more they feel they have to conform to limited social norms of masculinity:

> According to conformity to masculine norms theory, men who feel greater pressure to conform to societal expectations of "what it means to be a man" are at greater risk for negative psychological functioning. Conformity to masculine norms theory has identified a subset of dominant norms of traditional masculinity that are prevalent in American society: (a) Winning; (b) Emotional Control; (c) Risk-Taking; (d) Violence; (e) Power Over Women; (f) Playboy; (g) Self-Reliance; (h) Primacy of Work; and (i) Heterosexual Self-Presentation. Research in the psychological study of men and masculinity has demonstrated that conforming to

10. Putney, *Muscular Christianity*, 10, 206.

11. Recently the FCA has launched some new initiatives around "women's staff development" in order to "multiply the reach of the gospel . . . to female coaches and athletes." See Seward, "60 Years and Counting," 20. I am not sure exactly what this new initiative entails, but it sounds like somehow they have gotten a message that they have not been ministering to women adequately. I was actually the president of my high school's FCA chapter in the 1980s. I remember several junctures during my involvement with FCA when I was confused about the mixed messages I got about how women's leadership was regarded.

traditional masculine norms can exact a cost on men and on others in men's lives.[12]

Aggression and violence are two of the main markers that this particular study tracks as a result of conformity to masculine norms. We are also learning as a culture that aggressive and violent behaviors are often tangled up with depression, addiction, and other life-diminishing realities.

Do sports like football require such limited constructions of masculinity and femininity in order to function well? Are such constricted spaces required for this American passion to thrive? There are clear signs in our contemporary moment in American culture that those same

> *Constrained gender performance and its detrimental effects are contributing to the decline in popularity of football today.*

constricted spaces may be what lead to the demise of football. Increasing research about head trauma from concussions, as well as more honest discussions about the physical and emotional toll that men who play football over the long haul endure, have encouraged our culture to start to ask questions.

Some of the most pressing and damaging questions to the world of football are coming not from the NFL, but from Pop Warner and Pee Wee football, as fewer parents want their kids to play football.[13] One ESPN survey said that 57 percent of parents are now less likely to allow their kids to play football, in light of recent findings about concussions.[14] Even some NFL players themselves are confessing that they are not encouraging their sons to play.[15] In our own family we have struggled with this question as well. Our son has interestingly enough chosen to play rugby, not football. Rugby is a sport that is rough, violent, and played without helmets or pads. We are encountering a very different culture around the sport, however, than what we routinely encounter in American football. One of the main differences is that there are women's rugby teams and girls play rugby on some of the

12. Steinfeldt et al., "Moral Atmosphere and Masculine Norms in American College Football," 343.

13. Barra, "America's Most Dangerous Football."

14. Lavigne, "Concussion News Worries Parents."

15. Ibid. Lavigne writes, "The concern comes from parents who could care less about the NFL and those who are rabid fans, which shouldn't be surprising considering some of the NFL's biggest stars, including former quarterback Kurt Warner and New York Jets linebacker Bart Scott, have said they don't even want their boys to play football."

teams against which my son has competed. And we have noticed in many situations that there is a broader continuum for how masculinity is defined and performed in rugby than in football. One emblem of that dynamic is the existence of openly gay players at the highest levels of rugby as opposed to football, which still has a tenacious silence around the presence of homosexual players, especially at the highest levels of the sport.[16]

If manning up means *unveiling the systemic distortions and contortions of sport that continue to prop up exclusionary and even abusive models of masculinity,* football provides us with an apocalypse worth our gaze. Its performance of gender stereotypes lies at the extremes and its sharp edges are becoming more and more visible to our collective awareness. A life-giving opportunity emerges from this increased visibility. When we see ourselves, when we see our gendered selves, in this apocalyptic light, we have a chance to face our fears. When it comes to gender what we fear the most might just be ambiguity. And when it comes to sports, we have often created gendered templates to facilitate the repetitive performance of gender that assures us we can avoid gender ambiguity altogether.

Surfacing fears gives us a chance to understand what we fear the most. Fear of ambiguity around gender roles tells us that we fear there is too much to lose in letting go of these rigid constructions of gender. The fraying edges around the world of football that are giving parents pause as they raise their children tells us that we also may have something to gain by making space for more real bodies, more complicated bodies. The trivialization of the complexity of human beings has never served humanity well. Stereotyping tends to make us all fly a little lower than we would otherwise. Will allowing for more of a continuum of human beings of both genders to take up space in a sport like football diminish who we are or what sports mean to us? Having the courage to let the truth emerge may just be what gives us the freedom to elevate our game beyond what seemed possible.

16. In 2014 Michael Sam became the first openly gay play to be drafted into the NFL. There was some conjecture leading up to the draft that his coming out prior to the draft would hurt his draft position.

5

White Lines

Only by committing ourselves to color-consciousness—meaning an awareness of the *consequences* of color in a historically white-dominated nation—can we even theoretically begin to alter those consequences.[1]

ICONS AND MIRRORS

SPORTS IN AMERICA GIVE us both icons and mirrors of race.

Jessie Owens winning four Berlin Olympics' gold medals is one of those iconic moments. Owens embodied the capacity to cross social boundaries and transform our collective imaginations. Owens dominated the field in his events in front of history's most notorious white supremist, Adolf Hitler. And America, with Owens on the medal platform, stood for something very different than a regime that made whiteness its organizing principle.

Many who have played organized sports in the last half-century will tell you that their sport was where they developed friendships across racial boundaries. In my own experience, as a track and field athlete, this space for boundary crossing was indeed substantive and life-giving. While these relational opportunities are important and a beautiful layer of sport's capacity to embody humanity's better angels, this chapter is not about this

1. Wise, *Colorblind*, 191.

interpersonal layer of sports. *The subtler question about race and sports circles around how sports carry the systemic marks of racism and privilege.* These systemic markers are important because they can be difficult to see and they are potent in their capacity to retrench our worst distortions around race. This apocalypse invites a shift away from looking to sports for civil rights iconography toward a closer scrutiny of how white culture and privilege have found a way to flourish in the world of sports.

It is easy to look at the world of revenue sports and believe that it is a space of racial equity, or even to assume that certain racial groups have an advantage. People often want to point to black achievement in sports like track and field, basketball, and football as evidence that there are biological differences in

> *There are no genetically based predispositions to athletic ability that are based on race. Race is not a biologically derived category; it is a socially derived category.*

the construction of black bodies that make them stronger, faster, quicker, more agile, and better fit for athletic achievement. Biological science and genetics actually paints a very different picture of physiological differences between racial groups. In fact, DNA tells us that there is very little genetic variation among the human race, and that there are no biological differences within the human species that occur along racial boundaries or identities.[2] Among the species that share this planet with us, we are one of the most homogenous of all.[3]

There is no biological advantage for athletic achievement that is based on racial identity. Contemporary science actually tells us that, when it comes to biology, there is no basis for anything like the category we call race. *Race is a socially constructed concept that is based on the social advantage of whiteness.* When society has tried to prop up racialized categories with scientific fact there is no solid ground on which to base it. These categories

2. The best documentary on race that I have seen is *Race—The Power of an Illusion.* It begins with a segment on biology and race. If you are a person who believes that there is a biological basis for race (even if you don't feel you attribute anything negative to the belief in biological differences between the races) this documentary is worth watching. A quote from the documentary's website: "*Race—The Power of an Illusion* questions the very idea of race as biology, suggesting that a belief in race is no more sound than believing that the sun revolves around the earth."

3. Any questions you might have about current science around race can be answered at the companion website to the above documentary (see note 2). There is also a rich bibliography of suggested reading you can do if you are interested in going deeper into these important scientific facts and what they mean for how we navigate race.

and the way we define them has always shifted and changed with what is at stake for the dominant group, namely whites.

These unsupported biological arguments based on race for athletic prowess have helped to create cultural assumptions and impressions about racialized advantage in athletics. These collective cultural assumptions circle mostly around the assumption that certain racial groups (namely blacks/African-Americans) share more of the spoils of the wealth generated in sports. Media images of glitzy black athletes with lavish spending habits are societal grist for the mill when it comes to the much-bemoaned fact that American culture has our priorities out of whack. Why are athletes paid so much? How can they be so greedy as to demand bigger and bigger contracts? The American conscience is troubled by such skewed values even as we spend billions of dollars on tickets, merchandise, television access, and more to watch these same players compete.

Americans do not tend to have the same squeamishness about the wealth of sports teams' owners as they do about the salaries of players. During our twelve years in the National Football League (NFL), I can at least report anecdotally that I can think of almost no one who ever commented on how wrong it was that owners enjoy so many of the spoils of NFL football revenue, while I have had countless conversations with people who are offended by how much money the players make.

A closer look at how the wealth and power is actually distributed in the big revenue sports in America actually reveals something quite different than conventional thinking assumes. In the NFL 65 percent of the players are black while 31 percent are white. The National Basketball Association (NBA) in 2011 reported that 78 percent of its players were African-American. In NCAA Division I football and basketball, blacks are a majority of the players (almost 46 percent in football, almost 61 percent in basketball). Many argue, therefore, that blacks have more of an opportunity than whites do in these revenue-producing sports to benefit financially at the highest levels.

While the NBA far outshines the NFL in the racial diversity all through the organization,[4] those who benefit the most financially from the world of sports are still disproportionally white. In all of the major professional revenue sports (NBA, NFL, MLB) there is only one African-American who

4. In 2011 53 percent of the coaches in the NBA were people of color with 47 percent of them being black, while the NFL in 2013 decreased the number of black head coaches from almost 15 percent to only 9 percent, that is, three of its thirty-two teams. See http://www.tidesport.org/RGRC/2012/2012_NBA_RGRC[1].pdf.

is majority owner of a team, Michael Jordan of the NBA Carolina Hornets. Seventy-eight percent of black NFL players are bankrupt within two years of their retirement, while 60 percent of NBA players are bankrupt within five years of their retirement.[5]

The marks of race and privilege do not stop with these more outward signs of poorly shared power and illusory financial equity—they also show themselves in unconscious stereotyping and gut reactions that we all have as spectators. For instance, one study shows that black players in the NFL are more likely to be penalized for excessive celebration. And the public's interpretation of black players who celebrated also tends to be more negative.[6]

A look at the racial demographics of NCAA sports also yields some telling information when the veil is lifted from the way race and privilege operate. The statistics stated above about the number of players who are people of color who participate in revenue sports is only part of the picture.[7] A contrast to the high percentage of players of revenue sports on college campuses who are black is the low number of head coaches and athletic administrators on those same campuses who are black. For the 2012 football season there were eighteen head football coaches who are black in the 125 Football Bowl Subdivision (FBS) schools. And 100 percent of the conference commissioners of the member conferences of these schools are white.[8] Nearly 98 percent of the presidents on those same campuses are white. And almost 85 percent of the athletic directors of those programs are white. Clearly there is not equity when it comes to access to the channels of power in big-time sports.

> *In 2012, 46 percent of FBS players were black, 14 percent of the head coaches were black, 100 percent of the conference commissioners were white, 98 percent of the presidents of those schools were white, and 85 percent of the athletic directors of those programs were white.*

There is growing support for acknowledging the particular ways that revenue-producing sports in college embody some troubling patterns of injustice. Historian Taylor Branch has given us one of

---

5. Crawley, "122 Teams."

6. Hall and Livingston, "The Hubris Penalty."

7. In NCAA Division I football almost 46 percent of the players are black. In NCAA Division I basketball almost 61 percent of the players are black. See http://sports.espn.go.com/ncaa/news/story?id=5901855.

8. Study conducted at the University of Central Florida Institute for Diversity and Ethics in Sport, http://www.bus.ucf.edu/sportbusiness/?page=1445.

the most revealing sources on this topic. He traces the history of the NCAA and the development of the term "student-athlete" in sobering detail. From his research he has come to see the treatment of college athletes through the lens of America's history of racial oppression and slavery—a non-paid labor force kept in check by regulations enforced by white-run institutions who benefit financially. Branch explains that he used to be a person who bristled at the thought of paying college athletes, but after taking a closer look he has come up with a very different conclusion. He writes:

> But after an inquiry that took me into locker rooms and ivory towers across the country, I have come to believe that sentiment blinds us to what's before our eyes. Big-time college sports are fully commercialized. Billions of dollars flow through them each year. The NCAA makes money, and enables universities and corporations to make money, from the unpaid labor of young athletes. Slavery analogies should be used carefully. College athletes are not slaves. Yet to survey the scene—corporations and universities enriching themselves on the backs of uncompensated young men, whose status as "student-athletes" deprives them of the right to due process guaranteed by the Constitution—is to catch an unmistakable whiff of the plantation. Perhaps a more apt metaphor is colonialism: college sports, as overseen by the NCAA, is a system imposed by well-meaning paternalists and rationalized with hoary sentiments about caring for the well-being of the colonized . . . The NCAA today is in many ways a classic cartel.[9]

This troubling reality is a haunting emblem of slavery's legacy.

These marks of white culture are prevalent in the mode of operation of big-time sports in both college and professional ranks—especially in those organizations and institutions where there is a greater concentration of athletes of color. In the world of football, for instance, not only is there is a gross imbalance of who occupies the roles of decision makers (team owners, athletic directors, general managers, NCAA officials, and head coaches to name a few) when we look for racial/ethnic diversity in those constituencies, but there are also numerous systems in place that help to concentrate financial benefit among those who are white.

In college football the majority of those playing at the Division I level are people of color and most of these players live under the poverty line

9. Branch, "The Shame of College Sports."

during their years playing college athletics. A recent study of every Division I football and basketball program reveals several startling findings:[10]

- In the 2009–2010 academic year the average annual scholarship shortfall (for out of pocket expenses) for "full scholarship" football (Football Bowl Subdivision—FBS) athletes was $3,222.

- Eighty-five percent of FBS schools leave their "full scholarship" football athletes who live on campus under the federal poverty line. For those who live off campus, that percent rises to eighty-six percent.

- The football and basketball players at the bottom of these statistics (the poorest third) live between $3000–$5000 below the federal poverty in an academic year while these same players generated (combined football and basketball) over $30 million in revenues from their play.

This study tells us that the term "full" scholarship is misleading. Any compensation or stipend that players receive to cover the normal out-of-pocket expenses associated with college life falls short of providing most of these students with a livable financial situation as defined by the federal poverty line guidelines. The NCAA defines a full athletic scholarship as including "tuition and fees, room, board, and required course-related books."[11] The study compares this figure with the university-generated figures for cost of attendance. The shortfall is the resulting difference. Obviously, athletes from families with fewer economic resources will be at a pronounced economic disadvantage in this scenario. Athletes from privilege are able to more easily bridge the gap. Athletes from poverty are not.

Dr. Richard Southall, Director of the College Sport Research Institute, describes another layer of this privilege by tracing both the racial and economic demographics of how full scholarship funds are both generated and distributed. He says:

> [T]he majority of NCAA FBS football and DI men's basketball players (including those with the greatest market value) are African-American males who come disproportionately from lower-to-middle class socio-economic backgrounds, and the majority of expenditure (Olympic-sport) athletes are White athletes from middle-to-upper-class backgrounds, as reflected in the comments of the athletic director of a prominent FBS university to his athletic

10. Staurowsky and Huma, *The Price of Poverty in Bigtime College Sports.*
11. Ibid., 15.

council, that the median annual family income of Olympic-sport athletes at his university is $500,000.[12]

These statistics and findings reveal systems tenaciously protected in college sports that effectively draw white lines between athletes of privilege and athletes who arrive at college with an economic deficit. *As is often the case in American society overall, when these white lines are drawn between groups based on economic resources, people of color are often on the losing side of the equation.*

Universities receive millions of dollars from revenue sports—enough to fund whole athletic departments in some cases, and in other cases to fund even more of the universities' interests. In 2011–12 the NCAA reported its revenue as $871.6 million.[13] They report that "all but 4 percent of NCAA revenue is either returned directly to member conferences and institutions or used to support championships and programs that benefit student-athletes."[14] While most of the players who generate the bulk of this revenue stream (football and basketball players in Division I programs) live under the poverty line, Mark Emmert, president of the NCAA, reported a salary for 2010 of $1.6 million.

These numbers and disparities are clear. And these same disparities are even more complicated and troubled by the ways that the same players who live under the poverty line while they generate income for the NCAA and universities are strictly controlled about how they can be assisted by other sources of income. They cannot receive "benefits" like dinners out, clothes, gas money, or even rides to the airport from others without running the risk of committing NCAA violations in many cases. Some of the most serious violations come when players accept financial assistance from agents or those who represent agents. While we were at UNC a player fainted in the training room because he had not eaten for several days when the school's training table for football players was not open. He had sent his *per diem* home to help his family make ends meet. Another player was banned from NCAA sports for life because he took money from an agent. This player had originally taken money from the agent to pay his mother's heating bill.

12. Southall, "Rawlings Panel Remarks."

13. On the NCAA's website there is information about all financial information that they disclose. In 2011–12, 81 percent of their revenue stream came from their TV contract with Turner/CBS Sports. This was one year's revenue out of a fourteen-year deal worth $10.8 billion. See http://www.ncaa.org/about/resources/finances/revenue.

14. See http://www.ncaa.org/about/resources/finances/revenue.

Athletes are not only seriously penalized for contact with agents, but agents themselves are guilty of a felony offense in forty-two states if they engage in a business relationship with players before they become professionals. The Uniform Athletes Agent Act (2000) was encouraged by the NCAA and universities to up the ante against agents and their representatives who try to make contact with players while they are still playing in college.[15] Making this kind of contact a felony offense is intended to scare agents from inducing players to be clients before they turn pro. There is a movement afoot to extend this statute to include financial advisors and marketing people. I have not been able to find any other example of a professional track where it labeled as "misconduct," much less a felony offense, for someone to be courted by companies or headhunters while they are in college or to enlist the services of financial advisors or agents. For instance, a student studying finance could receive a paid trip to a social event if a financial institution is recruiting them. Or a candidate for a position in a law firm could be treated to things that would incentivize them to take that job. If an engineering student came up with an idea and had it patented while a student at a university, she would be able to reap the benefits of her intellectual property. Why are athletes singled out and treated as a different class of people when it comes to being free to benefit from the revenue their labor generates and to employ those who can help them do that?[16]

WHITE LINES

In this apocalyptic gaze the fact that the majority of these revenue-producing, unpaid athletes are black is of particular interest. It is not the "just so happens to be that way" reality that many whites would like to think it is. The apocalypse of sports and race does not show us as symbols of access and equity; this apocalypse reveals marks of our most chronic patterns of racially derived

Whereas whiteness is not perceived as a racial category, other categories are; whereas a white neighborhood is a "normal" neighborhood, a black neighborhood is "racially segregated."

—*Eduardo Bonilla-Silva*

15. See http://www.uniformlaws.org/Committee.aspx?title=Athlete%20Agents%20Act.

16. Former Duke basketball player and current ESPN analyst Jay Bilas laid out this issue clearly in his speech to the Rawlings Panel at UNC in April 2013.

inequity in America. When the veil is lifted we see sports as another example of an American system created by the dominant culture that benefits the dominant culture. There are many ways that the world of big-time sports embodies the marks of white culture in its systems, its values, and it practices. Many of these habits are things that do not show up as "white values" because these norms are generated from a dominant culture that has never understood itself as having a race or culture.

Sociologist Eduardo Bonilla-Silva explains that in our post civil rights American context a "new racism" has emerged.[17] He describes this as "a new kinder and gentler white supremacy" that maintains systemic white privilege "socially, economically, and politically through institutional, covert, and apparently nonracial practices."[18] Bonilla-Silva tracks the subtleties of this new racism by naming a "white habitus" that is nurtured and maintained in white institutions and lifestyles. This white habitus is "a racialized, uninterrupted socialization process that *conditions* and *creates* whites' racial taste, perceptions, feelings, and emotions and their views on racial matters."[19] White "color-blind styles of talking about race without naming it" are a product of this white habitus.

There are some common frames that Bonilla-Silva has found in his extensive interviews with whites around issues of race that characterize this color-blind style of talking about race without naming it. These frames serve to normalize inequities by ignoring the effects of generations of discrimination based on race in America. While these frames are familiar parts of everyday life in America and surface in the life of many institutions, from schools, to churches, to our justice system, these habits of talking, thinking and perceiving are not seen in racial terms by most whites. These frames help define the contours of white privilege.[20] And when it comes to sports there is even another layer of camouflage because we tend to see sports as a symbol of access and even advantage for people of color, namely blacks and African-Americans. The prevalence of participation in revenue sports by people of color can serve to shroud discrimination even further. The double layer obfuscation makes the way the NCAA investigation at UNC unfolded an important subject of our scrutiny.

17. Bonilla-Silva, *Racism without Racists*, 183.

18. Ibid.

19. Ibid., 104.

20. The common working definition for white privilege comes from Peggy McIntosh. McIntosh, *White Privilege and Male Privilege*, 1.

How did white privilege surface in the NCAA investigation at UNC and why does it matter? With the help of Bonilla-Silva's framework of *white habitus* as well as the work of Maggie Potapchuk, who names characteristics of *white culture* in order to better bring into focus the dynamics of whiteness, we can lift the veil on the UNC investigation. This apocalypse can sharpen our gaze at some of the tenacious patterns of privilege and

> *"White privilege is an invisible package of unearned assets which I can count on cashing in each day, but about which I was 'meant' to remain oblivious."*
>
> —*Peggy McIntosh*

power at work in college athletics today. While some of the dynamics of UNC's investigation may be unique to UNC's culture and context, many of the institution's strategies were suggested and encouraged by the NCAA. Bonilla-Silva's categories of abstract liberalism, cultural racism, and the minimization of racism help to surface these white lines.

The first frame Bonilla-Silva lifts up is that whites tend to use an *"abstract liberalism"* to apply values and norms to race matters in a non-racialized way. For instance, the values of equal opportunity, individualism, and merit may be elicited as priorities for systems to be fair all the while masking the profound deficits in black communities and lives due to the effects of generations of discrimination.[21] The use of values like individualism helps to create common patterns of blame and accountability that fail to explore the systemic cultures of institutions. White culture focuses on individuals, not groups. Individuals are responsible for their own behavior, apart from systems and institutional cultures.[22] In this emphasis on individuals there is little room for critical awareness of how systems put certain groups at a disadvantage and compromise individual agency and opportunity.

This framing of issues with individualism was one of the organizing principles of the UNC football investigation.[23] The rhetoric of school offi-

---

21. For an excellent explication of the long term effects of discrimination on people of color in America, see Wise, *Colorblind*.

22. Potupchuk, "White Culture Handout."

23. The question of how race and white privilege played a role in the UNC football investigation was posed to me during a lecture I gave (via Skype) to a class on Sports Ethics at the University of Washington's Center for Leadership in Athletics in the spring of 2013. And this information was also the topic one of my blog posts on the *Feminism and Religion* blog (www.feminismandreligion.com), to which I am a quarterly contributor. See http://feminismandreligion.com/2013/04/30/feminism-and-football-by-marcia-w-mount-shoop/.

cials over and over again emphasized holding individuals accountable. And their actions and processes certainly played that principle out clearly. Individual players were singled out because of suspicions of potential NCAA violations—some for attending a party hosted by a sports agent and others for alleged academic improprieties. All of these young men were black and many were punished before any guilt had been proven. Some were later found not to have done anything wrong but had already been punished, some in ways that changed their lives forever.[24]

The tendency to focus on individuals as the main object of accountability and punishment helps to surface a sinister twist in the NCAA's system of regulation and enforcement. The NCAA puts the power in the hands of institutions to determine guilt or innocence with no due process in place for those accused to be heard fairly. The NCAA manual is built on player eligibility, yet here is no NCAA process in place for players that affords them a hearing or the exercise of other rights when they have been accused of a violation.

The NCAA advises member universities about whether something is a violation or not. Member universities decide whether to rule a player ineligible or not after receiving the advice of the NCAA. If the school chooses not to impose any penalty on a player who the NCAA feels is guilty of a violation, then the university runs the risk of being sanctioned for playing an ineligible player. Unless the university has a system of due process in place for athletes, there is no opportunity for an athlete to plead guilty or innocent or engage in a fair hearing.

A system of accountability based on holding individuals accountable that has no due process for individuals is nothing short of abusive. When former North Carolina Supreme Court Justice Robert Orr, who represented Devon Ramsay after the NCAA ruled him permanently ineligible, asked Jennifer Henderson, the head of NCAA compliance, where in the 400-plus pages of the NCAA manual was there anything about players' rights, Ms. Henderson responded by saying, "That's a good question."[25]

Devon's case is a perfect example of the arbitrariness of the NCAA's system. Devon was ruled ineligible by UNC on the advice of the NCAA due to a suspicion that he had received improper assistance on a paper he

24. Devon Ramsay's story is just one example. There have been several stories written about Devon, including on my blog; see http://marciamountshoop.com/2011/11/25/calling-audibles-part-viii-face-time/.

25. Phone conversation with Robert Orr, January 18, 2014, and email correspondence, January 23, 2014.

wrote for a class. This accusation surfaced even though the paper he had written that was in question was nowhere to be found (it had been written a few years before the allegations were made). The email that raised suspicion between Devon and UNC tutor, Jennifer Wiley, included Wiley's suggestion that Devon might move a couple of sentences to another part of his paper. Devon couldn't remember if he had moved the sentences or not. The NCAA said that UNC should assume that he did it and that he was ineligible. When the university asked the NCAA if the games Devon had already missed was enough of a penalty (UNC had benched Devon "just in case" during the investigation), the NCAA said he was permanently ineligible because it was an academic offense, even though there was no proof of an offense. According to UNC officials if Devon wanted to appeal the NCAA ruling, then he first had to admit guilt. His attorney refused to admit guilt and chose to go a legal route to seek reinstatement through legal documentation of "new evidence" in the case. Devon was reinstated because he was found not guilty after Mr. Orr's legal intervention.

Devon and other players were told by UNC officials when the investigation began that "if you are not guilty, you don't need a lawyer." That was clearly not the case for Devon. And it is clearly not the case for any athlete caught up in a system where there is no due process for the individuals who are held accountable by the system. And the system was stacked against these eighteen young men at UNC in no small part due to the obliviousness of the white power brokers who were in charge of the process. The University and NCAA persist in their hyper focus on individuals while they ignore clear evidence of disadvantage in the system for particular groups of people, namely, young black men.

Even after information surfaced several months into the investigation about systemic issues in the area of academic advising of athletes at UNC, former Athletic Director Dick Baddour still spoke publicly about a "few bad individuals who almost brought down the University of North Carolina."[26] The individuals Baddour was referring to were players, not anyone in the power structure at UNC. This prevalent sentiment of blaming particular players for the entire situation was expressed to my family and to me countless times during the investigation and its aftermath. Many people said how upset they were that UNC's reputation was being tarnished just because of a "few bad apples." Others said it was wrong and unfair that our family

26. Radio interview with David Glenn on 99.9 the Fan, March 2012.

had to be uprooted and move away because a few players were "greedy and undisciplined."[27]

All of these responses failed to take into account the complex set of factors at work in the situation. These factors included everything from common institutional practices, to bad advising by UNC employees, to a lack of due process, and more. The fact that everyone who was being accused was black and everyone doing the accusing was white never surfaced as an official concern of the university. The investigation focused on individual actions rather than the possibility of systemic problems.

Another frame in Bonilla-Silva's description of white habitus is *"cultural racism."* This frame chalks up the problems endemic in largely black communities to deficits in black culture. For instance, tendencies toward violence, poor work ethic, loose family structures, lack of education, cycles of poverty, and government dependence are characterized as aspects of black culture, or sometimes it is labeled a "culture of poverty."[28] In other words, this frame sees the social ills that are rampant in many largely black communities as the fault of those who bear the brunt of their effects rather than the result of systemic racism and discrimination.

We can accent this cultural racism frame with two of the characteristics in Maggie Potapchuk's description of white culture. First, white culture creates hierarchies around certain behaviors and labels others as deviant or dangerous. And second, white culture defines what is considered normal—it creates the standard for judging values. Examples of these characteristics

---

27. The entire football coaching staff was eventually fired. One coach, John Blake, was suspected of unethical behavior and potentially committing NCAA violations through his friendship with an agent. He resigned early in the investigation. Head Coach Butch Davis was fired in August 2011, even though he was not named in any of the allegations. None of the remaining coaches were accused of any wrongdoing. They were a part of Head Coach Butch Davis' staff and were let go after the 2011 season to make room for a new head coach to hire his staff. This kind of mass firing is not unusual in the world of football. One unusual aspect, however, in this particular situation was that not one coach was retained on the new staff. Some people in the university's administration said that the school just needed a "fresh start" in order to "restore the integrity of the football program."

28. Tim Wise systematically dismantles the "cultural of poverty thinking" of progressive white liberals in *Colorblind*, with statistics about everything from birth rates to the likelihood of receiving government assistance to educational achievement. These statistics disprove any correlation between the things like births out of wedlock, receiving government assistance, high school graduation rates, and race. Wise, *Colorblind*, 126–32. The quote in the text box above is from his essay "Default Position," in *Speaking Treason Fluently*, 245.

are how we define things like "good parenting," children who have "good manners," and how we understand the propriety of things like showing emotion, avoiding conflict, and what it means to make other people feel comfortable. This frame was clearly apparent during the UNC investigation with the commonly used rhetoric of "the Carolina Way."

The "Carolina Way" was a phrase coined by former UNC basketball coach, Dean Smith. It is a frequently used phrase at UNC to signal the right way to do things and the way things are done at "Carolina." There isn't a set definition for this turn of phrase; the

> *Just because the norm is not racially named, doesn't mean it isn't racialized.*
>
> —*Tim Wise*

UNC website indicates these are "words we understand so well, they often don't require defining."[29] A marketing video on the same website interviews people on campus for their understanding of the Carolina Way. Answer range from "always treat everyone with respect" to words like "integrity and excellence." Others described the Carolina Way as "embracing all people," an "exceptional attitude," and being a "good, generous, and thoughtful person; being a good individual." Another person on the video described the Carolina Way as, "a part of you, a culture."

Over and over again during the NCAA investigation UNC officials explained that they were proceeding with the investigation "the Carolina Way," which meant full compliance and cooperation with the NCAA's wishes. And over and over again, the players who were accused of wrongdoing were described as not doing things the Carolina Way. What exactly this categorizing meant was difficult to parse out even for those of us closely involved with the situation. Sometimes it seems like the Carolina Way was about always following the rules or never being on the wrong side of the NCAA. Other times it seemed to be about a particular understanding of manners or propriety. Yet other times it was harder to figure out. Overall the message seemed to be the institution came first and any individual who threatened the "good name" of the institution was not really a part of the community.

A member of the UNC athletic administration said to John and me in a private conversation that he had decided long before the NCAA investigation began that one of the players involved in the investigation was not

---

29. See the University of North Carolina website: http://giving.unc.edu/why-give/make-an-impact/gifts-at-work/video/CCM3_035293.

someone who he wanted to wear a Carolina jersey. He decided this because the player kicked a ball into the stands after scoring a touchdown during a game. This administrator explained that this kind of behavior is not the Carolina Way. About other players on the football team who were involved in the investigation this same administrator said they did not belong at Carolina because he had heard that they cursed at coaches during practice. When John explained that cursing is a pretty common occurrence on football fields and that coaches address those issues with players when the cursing is disrespectful or problematic, this administrator said again that this was not the way things were done at Carolina.

His norms for appropriate behavior could not expand to include expressions of familiarity, humor, emotion, frustration that were different than those he valued and counted as endemic to life at UNC. For this administrator not cursing is the required norm for being respectable and worthy of inclusion in the Carolina community. If cursing, however, were grounds for removal from the community, most of the white players would be guilty, too. For players and coaches, cursing may be something they use in lots of different ways, but it is well within their norms for how they speak and relate to one another. The Carolina Way was the malleable norm this administrator called on to label certain behavior unacceptable when, in other instances, he might not want to make that an absolute depending who was doing the cursing.

This murky demeanor called the Carolina Way, which was apparently understood by those with power in the institution, provides the dominant culture with a way to draw lines between who belongs there and who does not. And the values that define what those ways of being and behaving are is a moving target that can be stretched and molded to fit any situation in which outsider status needs to be established. *The dominant culture defines propriety (the Carolina Way). Different ways of interacting or showing emotion, different life experiences and ways of navigating conflict, were seen as dangerous, devious, and outside the bounds of acceptable behavior.*

Such an arbitrary dynamic mirrors the United States Supreme Court's circular arguments during the twentieth century about what makes someone white. In the ultimate case ruling on the category of whiteness it finally said the Court did not need to define whiteness because any reasonable person knows what it is. The Court shifted its definitions of who was and wasn't white from case to case to fit the needs of the dominant culture at the time. When people of color who fit previous definitions the Court had ruled on for whiteness appealed to the Court for citizenship the Court would only make the definition more elusive and incoherent.[30] The end result was a pronouncement that "the average man knows perfectly well" what whiteness is when he sees it.[31]

During the UNC investigation it was clear that the eighteen players under suspicion for committing violations were widely assumed by the community to be guilty before being proven so. And many of them were quickly cast as interlopers, outsiders, and cheaters. The campus newspaper published mug-shot-like pictures of all of the players before there had been any determination of guilt or innocence.[32] It was common to hear comments like "They are sullying the good name of the University of North Carolina," "They don't know how to act," and "They should be more grateful just to be at UNC." These are all feelings that were directly communicated to us from various officials at UNC as well as others in the community. And certainly these sentiments were alive and well in the constant Internet chatter of some UNC fans and alumni.[33] The *Raleigh News & Observer* intentionally did not print stories that would depict the players in a positive light because their readers were not sympathetic to the players.[34]

This orientation toward the players only became clearer in how the process unfolded. Players were prohibited from playing in games "just in case" they did something wrong. Some of them missed an entire season and then were found to have either not committed any violations or to have committed such a minor violation that the commensurate penalty would not have involved missing multiple games or even any games. Devon

30. *United States v. Bhagat Singh Thind,* 261 U.S. 204 (1923).

31. Justice George Southerland in the Court's decision in the Thind case. See http://www.pbs.org/rootsinthesand/i_bhagat2.html.

32. "Connecting the Dots," *The Daily Tar Heel.*

33. A quick trip through some of the most commented on posts in my *Calling Audibles* blog series can give you a taste of these attitudes, particularly my post "The Anatomy of the Asterisk." See http://marciamountshoop.com/2012/07/26/calling-audibles-part-xxiii-the-anatomy-of-the-asterisk/.

34. In an email exchange I had with Robert Orr (January 24, 2014), he described the conversation with the *News & Observer* (*N&O*) as follows: "After Devon was cleared of any wrongdoing, the sports reporter for the *N&O* and I discussed the need for a comprehensive story about Devon's case emphasizing that he had been determined to have not violated any NCAA rule. Weeks went by and no story appeared. I eventually ran into the reporter and asked why no story had been written. He replied, 'There won't be a story. My editors don't think the players are sympathetic.'"

Ramsay and Deunta Williams are both clear examples of this guilty before proven innocent approach. Both Devon and Deunta missed multiple games for what turned out to be no reason. Both Devon and Deunta were irreparably disadvantaged by the games they missed. Both solid NFL prospects, neither was able to make it into the league after the deficits created by the investigation. Players who remained at UNC after the new coaching staff arrived told us that UNC athletic staff talked to the football team at the beginning of the season and flashed up pictures of many of the players who were accused during the scandal. The staff members told the current players, "Don't be like them."

The fact that all of the players who were named in the scandal were black, the coach who was accused of wrongdoing was black, the department at the university that was punished was the African-American studies program, was all never officially examined as cause for a closer look at institutional practices. From UNC's perspective, this process was color-blind and the racial identity of those accused was incidental. Such color-blind procedures are, as is proven again and again in American culture, not color-neutral. An opportunity to investigate what about UNC's culture keeps white ways propped up and creates disadvantages for people of color was not of interest to those with the power to make such decisions. Instead the university has continued its quest to raise academic standards and tighten admissions policies to assure that this kind of situation will not happen again.[35]

All of these patterns of decision-making that discourage diversity and inclusion continue to be made despite mission statements about the university's commitment to diversity and inclusion.[36] The hierarchies of acceptable behavior were clearly established in a way that put certain groups at a disadvantage. In a country where white ways and mentalities have dominated, it is never a coincidence when so many people of color are on the losing end of a situation like the one at UNC. Institutional scrutiny bypassed its

35. See, for instance, Curliss, "Thorp: UNC's Standards for Athletes Will Rise."

36. On UNC's website they explain their commitment to diversity and inclusion as follows: "The University of North Carolina at Chapel Hill has a long-held tradition of striving for excellence. A critical element for any twenty-first century educational institution is a diverse and inclusive community. The vision of the Office of Diversity and Multicultural Affairs is to build and sustain an inclusive campus community and to foster a welcoming climate that values and respects all members of the University community. The mission of the Office affirms the University's commitment to diversity as a critical element of academic excellence." See http://www.unc.edu/diversity/.

own habits and practices and focused on separating out aberrant individuals. And former Athletic Director Dick Baddour said confidently after the NCAA handed down their final word on the investigation, "There's still a Carolina way. And the way we did this investigation—it's my strong belief it was the Carolina way. We set out four guiding principles when we started. And number four was we would be better as a result of this."[37]

"Being better" can mean a lot of things and whether UNC is better for this investigation is certainly debatable. From the perspective of diversity there are several areas in which UNC is not better, including a decreased amount of diversity on the coaching staff and on the athletic department staff.[38] The only thing that is clear is that those who are within the dominant culture at UNC are the ones who get to say what better is.

The final frame Bonilla-Silva employs that helps us unveil the marks of race and privilege in sports is the *"minimization of racism."* This minimization assumes that the systems of justice and merit in American culture are fair and that discrimination is no longer a going concern. We can accent this frame with two more of Potapchuk's characteristics of white culture. Decision-making reflects cultural assumptions about power over others. Those less affected by decisions and rules are the ones who define problems and solutions. That is, those who stand to benefit and not to be disadvantaged by the system are the ones deciding on and enforcing the rules. Those most disadvantaged by the rules have little or no power in making them.

This way of exercising power over others often lends itself to either/ or thinking. Such either/or thinking creates polarities between good and bad, right and wrong, appropriate and inappropriate, and compliance and non-compliance. You are either conforming to our standards, or you are not. In the aftermath of the NCAA investigation, UNC has explained that is has a "zero-tolerance" policy when it comes to those who commit NCAA violations.[39] This either/or policy continues to put young men of color at a disadvantage.

The university's treatment of wide receiver Dwight Jones shows us just how this zero tolerance policy works. Dwight was not involved in the

37. Carter, "UNC's Thorp Calls NCAA Sanctions 'Painful.'"

38. The football coaching staff went from having four full-time coaches who are black to two. The athletic department has increased the number of white males on its payroll. All of the recent promotions in the athletic department were given to white males.

39. For more on this case, see my blog post "The Anatomy of the Asterisk": http://marciamountshoop.com/2012/07/26/calling-audibles-part-xxiii-the-anatomy-of-the-asterisk/.

NCAA investigation. He did everything he was asked to do on the team and was one of the best wide receivers ever to play for UNC. At the end of his senior season a family member put a picture of Dwight on Facebook to advertise a birthday party for Dwight that was set to occur in January after he would no longer be a student at UNC. The University ruled Dwight ineligible for the bowl game in agreement with NCAA advice because Dwight's cousin was charging a cover charge into the party to cover the costs of the place where the party would be held in Burlington, North Carolina. The fact that Dwight's picture was used for a party where there would be a cover charge was an NCAA violation—the commercialization of his image.

Dwight had the picture removed when he was told by UNC officials that it was a violation. UNC officials asked him to sign a statement they had written that said he done things that he had not done. With John's assistance, Dwight opted not to sign the statement and to discuss the situation with an attorney. With the help of attorney Robert Orr, Dwight drafted a statement that he would sign and his eligibility was restored. He was able to compete in the bowl game. Dwight then finished the season and began preparing for the draft. He did not attend the party that his cousin ended up having in January. When the university found out that the party did occur they called Dwight just a few days before the NFL pro-day at UNC and told him he was not welcome because of their zero-tolerance policy.[40] Dwight, no longer at student at UNC, had no opportunity for recourse or to even make other plans. Even though the university had known it was going to do this for several weeks, it did not inform Dwight

> *Those most disadvantaged by the rules have little or no power in making them.*

until just a few days before. Dwight was not drafted. One is left wondering what the zero tolerance policy is really about at UNC. Zero tolerance of family members who do things we don't want them to do? Zero tolerance of being accused of an NCAA violation that you didn't actually commit? This abuse of power, this lack of due process, this arbitrary way of putting players in their place carries with it layers of intimidating messages. And because these arbitrary actions were all visited on black players, being guilty until proven innocent at UNC if you are black is one of the messages. To the white powers that be, race has nothing to do with it.

40. NFL pro days on college campuses are those days when NFL scouts come and watch potential signees work out.

This minimization of racism coupled with particular paradigms of how power is used creates situations ripe for people of color to be at a disadvantage. The effects of generations of discrimination are dismissed, explained away as caused by other things (like black culture, as described above), and not taken into account in how things like fairness, respect, and justice are understood and preserved. There is an assumed obviousness to what's right and what's wrong; conformity to those standards and cooperation with the powers that be are the behaviors that are rewarded. There is no space for a critical questioning of power structures; there is no legitimacy in not trusting the system to work. Everything is taken at face value, that it is what it says it is.

This frame and these characteristics surfaced in the UNC investigation in the university's orientation toward the NCAA and in its unwillingness to provide legal advocates for the players. The university promised full compliance and cooperation with the NCAA despite research and published material from one of the University's own alumni, Taylor Branch, that raises serious questions about the ethics and the fairness of the NCAA particularly when it comes to young men of color.

Dick Baddour's statements to the press and to the football staff and players during the investigation focused on the university's commitment to full cooperation with the NCAA.[41] Baddour explained that this full compliance meant not talking openly about the investigation, giving the NCAA everything that it asked for, and making sure that when the investigation was over that the NCAA would have good things to say about UNC.[42] "I am going to do what they ask me to do. [It is important to] stay within the process." This was Baddour's stated approach.

Baddour and others who were on the team who led the investigation assumed that if they followed the rules everyone would be treated fairly. They assumed the system worked. Members of the compliance staff and others in the athletic department instructed players not to seek legal representation. Various players were given a host of reasons why retaining legal counsel was either impossible or a bad idea. One member of the staff told players that they would appear more guilty if they got an attorney. Still others told them that they weren't allowed to get an attorney because it would be an NCAA violation to get a *pro bono* attorney if they weren't able to pay

41. Dick Baddour, interview with WRAL, August 12, 2010; see http://www.wral-sportsfan.com/unc/video/8129891/#/vid8129891.

42. Friedlander, "UNC Decides to Lawyer Up."

the full fees. And still others were told, "If you didn't do anything wrong then you don't need an attorney."[43]

Devon Ramsay's case shows us how these assumptions of fairness did not prove to be true as the investigation unfolded. And Devon will perhaps never be able to shake the "academic fraud" label that still follows him even though he did nothing wrong. The system was not fair. The system did not work. The process put players, particularly eighteen player who were people of color, at a disadvantage. Policies and procedures that benefited the university were directly harmful and unjust for the players most affected by the investigation. Those who were least affected by the procedures were the ones with the power to determine how the process played out. UNC officials maintain that race had nothing to do with how things played out. Their policies were color-blind. The results show who is disadvantaged when institutions ignore the systemic dynamics of race and privilege. Without a color-conscious approach, the dominant culture retains a clear advantage.[44]

Well after the NCAA handed down its verdict and UNC fans had moved on with a new coaching staff and most of the players involved gone from the team, Chancellor Holden Thorp appointed a panel to "consider the role of athletics at Carolina."[45] The Rawlings panel consists of five individuals, all but one of them are white.[46] None of them are coaches and none of them are athletes. I attended an event in which panel members heard from designated speakers—all of them white, and all of them men except for one woman. None of the speakers were coaches and none of the speakers were players. Both of these constituencies were a prominent part of the topic of conversation. Those least affected by the findings of this panel's work have the most power to affect its outcomes. Those most affected by

43. All of these anecdotes were told to John and me directly by players who were a part of the investigation.

44. Tim Wise ends *Colorblind* with a chapter titled "Illuminated Individualism: A Paradigm for Progressive Color-Consciousness." He explains, "Only by committing ourselves to color-concsiousness—meaning an awareness of the *consequences* of color in a historically white-dominated nation—can we even theoretically begin to alter [the] consequences [of racism]." Wise, *Colorblind*, 191. Eduardo Bonilla-Silva puts it a little differently. He invites people serious about healing the wounds of race to understand themselves not simply as "not racist" but instead as "anti-racist." He attributes this idea to sociologist Eileen O'Brien. Bonilla-Silva, *Racism without Racists*, 15.

45. See http://www.unc.edu/chan/chancellors/thorp_holden/040113-rawlings-panel.php.

46. See http://rawlingspanel.web.unc.edu/.

this panel's work and recommendations were not at to the table and were not even a part of the discussion.[47]

These frames of white habitus and white culture conceal the realities of white dominance and interpret the effects of racialized discrimination, not in terms of race, but through the lens of non-racialized paradigms. White privilege cultivates a way of seeing and navigating the world that allows race to recede from white consciousness even as race profoundly informs the way the world is interpreted and navigated. More importantly, this white consciousness profoundly informs how power is used and distributed and how institutions and their policies, procedures, and cultures are formed.

(E)RACE(ING) THE LINES

Habitus is not simply a habit; it is a disposition, a tendency, an outlook and attitude. Habitus cultivates in us a susceptibility to certain behaviors, assumptions, and intuitions.[48] Habitus can even develop into and form particular physical characteristics and reactions, cultivating in us tendencies toward particular kinds of reactions of feeling and judgment.[49] Surfacing the dynamics of white culture at work in college sports creates an opportu-

---

47. In an email correspondence with Chancellor Thorp in which I pointed out how problematic it was that there were not players or coaches or people of color who spoke to the panel or who are on the panel, he responded, "I agree with you that race and privilege should be part of the conversation. Interestingly, some of the people that I invited who could have spoken about that weren't able to attend. Richard Southall did touch on it in discussing the difference between Olympic and revenue sports." Email correspondence, April 25, 2013. While the chancellor acknowledged that race and privilege should be a topic of conversation, those issues were not enough of a priority to assure voice and representation of those who could speak to it even when a few people were unable to attend. Surely the profound effects of discrimination and racism and privilege were minimized if having these perspectives represented was not made a requirement for how the panel was composed and did its work.

48. In my book, *Let the Bones Dance*, I have a full description of habitus and disposition.

49. Bonilla-Silva describes "styles of color-blindness" in certain "linguistic manners and rhetorical strategies" common among whites he interviewed about matters of race. These five "stylistic aspects" of color-blindness include avoidance of direct racial language, "verbal parachutes" like "I am not a racist" and "I have black friends," projection (e.g., blacks are the ones who are racist), diminutives (e.g., it's a "little" frustrating that affirmative action favors blacks over whites), and verbal incoherence when asked about the most difficult issues. Bonilla-Silva, *Racism without Racists*, 53–73.

nity for the intentional development of new habits of behavior and institutional practice.

While the NCAA and institutions like UNC may be oblivious to the racialized (white) quality of their policies and practices, an honest and earnest apocalypse gives us information we cannot deny. *While there is no one person to blame, while we do not find the equivalent of Ku Klux Klan members at the helm of these institutions, and while those in power may even be governed by good intentions, there is more to cultivating just systems and thriving communities than good intentions and individual accountability.*

The tenacity with which the NCAA and institutions like UNC hold on to their hallowed modes of operation tells us that there is more at stake than meets the eye. What might happen if those with power in big-time sports engaged in a period of collective soul searching around the dynamics of race in sports? There is a system in place that results in clear disadvantages along racial lines. If we surfaced these white lines and looked at them with humility and honesty, what space might be cleared for new habits of mind and heart to emerge? Color-consciousness in big-time sports can open up new territory for equity and due process. Color-consciousness can create the conditions necessary for new iconography of race and sports to spring forth in true colors that reflect and refract real lived situations.

The demonic distortions of generations of racism were formed and are fed by white obliviousness. These same distortions are what create rulebooks that are too thick for the average person to lift. These same distortions are what channel huge amounts of resources into enforcement of rules and regulations. And it is these distortions that create the house of cards that injustice builds. I wonder how tired the white power brokers are of scrambling to maintain this house of cards and the white lines that define its mystique. When it comes to race and college sports, the apocalypse can liberate more than those held back by the white lines; it can also free those who work so hard to maintain them.

6

Higher Learning

Sports in American universities are a powerful source of ethical training both for participants and spectators. Contemporary collegiate sports, however, also pose a real challenge to the ethical mission of the university.[1]

BASIC TRAINING

A college degree is a valuable thing in our society. And the aspiration to go to college is something we encourage in our youth. Going to college is about education, yes, but it is also about cultivating access to opportunity, developing one's identity, and growing in one's capacity for active and constructive citizenship in the world. Universities boast lofty goals around all of these aspects of human growth and development. And these institutions seek to distinguish themselves as places that encourage and help form people who will make the world a better place.

In the midst of these lofty goals and higher learning there lies a uniquely American tension created by the spectacle of revenue sports inhabiting the hallowed halls of academia. And the common narrative that has come along with this tension for decades is that this strange coupling poses deep ethical and moral challenges to the treasured values of American academic institutions. The laments from university campuses and from

1. Gillespie, "Players and Spectators," 312.

society at large about the excesses of big-time sports often describe a battle of the wills almost cosmic in scope between academics and athletics. The Knight Commission on Intercollegiate Athletics was born in 1989 of this handwringing by academicians and college administrators.[2] The now familiar cry is that sports have become more important than academics; and this shift in priorities is a threat to the laudable purposes and goals of the American system of higher learning.

The injury, according to the common lament, is that academic integrity is eroded by the out of control popularity and importance of athletics. The rhetorical battle ensues from there—from this seemingly ill-fitted coupling, from this dysfunctional relationship. And this rhetoric has framed the long-time arguments about "what to do" about sports on campuses of higher learning. Despite all the talk, the revenues and growth of college sports have increased. Big-time sports has become even bigger and arguably even more important since the Knight Commission started its work. And there are few signs that there will ever be a radical rupture between big-time sports and higher education.[3]

I grew up and was formed as an athlete on a Division III college campus. The same stories of excess and cheating that gave rise to the Knight Commission's work, and the fact that I am the child of two academics, helped to form my early attitudes about the problems in college sports. I, too, joined the chorus of those who felt big-time sports was a threat to the

2. The Knight Commission was formed in 1989 and funded by the John S. and James L. Knight Foundation to recommend reform in intercollegiate athletics. The Commission was formed in response to several sports scandals during the 1980s. And the intention of the Commission is stated as follows on its website: "The Commission's initial goal was to recommend a reform agenda that emphasized academic values in an arena where commercialization of college sports often overshadowed the underlying goals of higher education. Since 1989, the Knight Commission on Intercollegiate Athletics has worked to ensure that intercollegiate athletics programs operate within the educational mission of their colleges and universities." See http://www.knightcommission.org/about.

3. Some people believe that the solution to the problem with having big-time revenue sports on university campuses would be solved by taking big-time sports out of university settings. This solution, as it is often suggested, could include the creation of minor leagues for the NBA and NFL. There are several reasons why I do not support this strategy. The most compelling reason not to support this strategy (in addition to the fact that it is immensely unrealistic and highly unlikely to happen) is the loss of diversity that this divorce would mean for universities. Between 2007 and 2010, 2.8 percent of undergraduate students were black and 57.1 percent of Division I football players were black. Harper, Williams, and Blackman, "Black Male Student-Athletes and Racial Inequities," 1.

academic integrity of the universities who let the boosters, athletic directors, and football and basketball coaches run their schools.[4]

And, as a Division III athlete, I understood the NCAA as a benevolent organization that supported and organized college athletics. I took for granted that membership in the NCAA meant colleges and universities were on the "up and up" when it came to sports. I was honored to be named the NCAA Woman of the Year for the State of Kentucky in 1991 and one of ten national finalists for the NCAA Woman of the Year for the entire NCAA athletic system that year also. Because of that award, my small liberal arts school in Kentucky, Centre College, got $10,000 for women's athletics.

For all these reasons, I was someone who not only believed in the worth and integrity of the NCAA, but gave it the benefit of the doubt when it came to stories of sports scandals on university campuses. I assumed the accused probably broke the rules and that the NCAA was there to make sure things were made right. It is probably the closest thing I had to a "good guys/bad guys" mentality. In just about every other facet of my life my experiences gave me more critical ways of looking at the dynamics of power and injustice.

LEARNING CURVE

White people are accountable for the ways in which we fail to hear and understand the needs and claims that other communities make upon us . . . White learning [often] comes at the expense of those already multiply harmed by white interpersonal and structural failures in perception, sensitivity, and justice.[5]

It was while John coached at the University of North Carolina that the veil was lifted for me, not simply on the NCAA's questionable tactics and its use and abuse of power, but on the distortions around how academicians and college administrators frame the problems with college sports. I emerged from that experience with a vastly different perspective. And this perspective has helped to surface a new framework for understanding both the

4. Full disclosure: I grew up in the heart of the Bluegrass State and a University of Kentucky basketball fan. I can remember driving by Wildcat Lodge, where the basketball players got to live, and discussing in our family car the problems with such excess and special treatment. Word on the street was that players didn't go to class and had tutors who did all of their work.

5. Vigen, "To Hear and to Be Accountable," 223.

promise and the peril of the marriage between higher learning and athletic competition, especially revenue-producing competition.

The apocalypse when it comes to higher learning and sports brings into focus a new paradigm for discerning where integrity is being threatened on university campuses. While many campuses have problems with academic integrity, sports is not the source or force behind that erosion. While many campuses have problems with financial responsibility and stewardship, sports are not the driving force behind those destructive habits and behaviors either.

The greatest threats to integrity on American campuses of higher learning are much more stealthy than the bright lights of big-time sports. These threats are so stealthy that they are often an accepted part of how we make sense of problems and how we even construct

> *The demonic blinds, it does not reveal.*

systems of reward and punishment. These threats are not outside forces infiltrating the hallowed halls of academia, they are part of the architecture that American society has constructed for learning, success, opportunity, and merit. And, for me, the most sobering realization is that these threats grow out of the very ways we work to construct and encourage relationships and community in these treasured spaces of our culture.

These distortions that erode the integrity of higher education are stealthy, and they are diffuse. The white lines described in the previous chapter snake through the deepest values and aspirations that have shaped American universities. The assumptions and cultural norms that help create the conditions ripe for the race-based disadvantage described in that chapter are intimately intertwined with some of the most sacred and accepted patterns of our collective consciousness around education and success. As with systemic racism and privilege, there is no one person to blame; there is no one problem to solve. Instead the lifted veil around higher education shows us a diseased understanding more than a battle of good guys versus bad guys.

When redemption is our goal, discerning ways to critically gaze at such a dynamic is crucial. When distortion is so very prevalent, so very banal, it is harder to see and to accept. This banality makes these patterns and paradigms even more difficult to change. It is hard for us to imagine a different way. And so, our higher learning here will be both difficult and delicate work; our collective learning curve is steep.

This chapter will not reveal a smoking gun that can be removed, but a generalized attitude and approach that calls out for reframing in order for redemption to have a fighting chance. And the character of redemption in the context of higher learning cultivates the conditions necessary for the things we say we want our institutions of higher learning to be the most— places that create informed citizens, realized potential, the capacity to contribute constructively to society, and vibrant communities of learning, innovation, and transformation. Our struggle is for all of these to become more viable possibilities than conditions on many university campuses currently allow.

We first need the eyes to see how our common ways of understanding may be blinding us to the actual sources of the problems from which we suffer. We continue to see scandal after scandal, more and more regulations and rules to try to stem the tide of the scandals, and more and more money being generated thus raising the stakes higher and higher in the politics of how these problems are addressed. Some of the very places we have turned to for making things right may be actually retrenching many of the habits of mind and patterns of behavior that are the sources of distortion in the first place.

Apocalypse calls on us time and time again to take a hard look at ourselves and at the cultures in which we live and move. Lifting the veil may reflect back some difficult truths, but those truths are revealed not for the purposes of punishment and destruction, but so that transformation might be set loose to unfold.

MYTH MAKING

> With increasing frequency (sports) threaten to overwhelm the universities in whose name they were established and to undermine the integrity of one of our fundamental national institutions: higher education.[6]

There are several shared assumptions that are played and replayed in the condemnation of college sports. Some of these assumptions focus on the athletes themselves and others on the behemoth of athletics itself. These assumptions will sound familiar to any who have paid attention to the academics versus athletics lament of the last several decades. The Knight

6. Knight Commission, *Keeping Faith with the Student Athlete*, 17.

Commission spells out many of these concerns in its original report: commercialization, lack of institutional control, special status for athletes and coaches of revenue sports, and the eroding of academic standards including the easing of admission standards to accommodate athletes.[7]

The Commission's answer to these problems is that presidents of universities (who have made up the bulk of the Commission since its inception) should be in charge of athletics. This restoration of power to the heads of the universities, the Commission asserted, would bring the values of athletics back in line with those of the university. And athletes would be understood not just as athletes, but as students first.[8] Their "One-Plus-Three" solution put presidents (One) in control of the Three: academic integrity, financial integrity, and accountability through certification.[9]

Presidential control, while it may have created modest change, did not stem the tide of growth and influence of athletics on university campuses. Since the Commission's 1991–1993 report, it has had two follow-up reports. By the Commission's own admission in their 2001 follow-up report, "the threat has grown rather than diminished."[10] It uses as evidence the number of academic institutions who were censured by the NCAA—more than fifty percent "broke the rules" indicating to the Commission that, "[w]rongdoing as a way of life seems to represent the status quo."[11]

Rule-breaking is a problematic way to take the pulse of what is happening with big-time sports on college campuses. Obviously increased regulation and enforcement (which has been the trajectory of the NCAA, at the encouragement of the Knight Commission and others) leads to increased rates of accusation and punishment. Using rule-breaking to gauge the nature of the "status quo" keeps our eyes on nonconformity to values that those with power are trying to normalize. It does not shift our gaze to deeper, more root conditions that can tell us more about what is actually going on. Recent studies have provided us with more substantive information about what is actually happening in the lives of athletes in big-time sports programs. And all of them indicate clear statistical proof of disadvantage

7. The 1991 Knight Commission Report, *Keeping Faith,* describes "The Problem" in the Reform section of its first report and emphasizes the "out of control" nature of athletics at schools that have big-time programs.

8. Ibid., 25.

9. Ibid.

10. Knight Commission, *Call to Action,* 11.

11. Ibid., 12.

for young men of color.[12] The Knight Commission never engaged these questions in any substantive way. Instead with each report it sharpened its critical posture toward athletic programs as too powerful, too brazen, too lucrative to be in a healthy partnership with the academic institutions that house them.

In its first follow-up report the Commission particularly laments the professionalization of sports. With the popularity of professional sports, college sports have stopped looking and acting like an amateur endeavor. The Commission states,

> Under the influence of television and the mass media, the ethos of athletics is now professional. The apex of sporting endeavor is defined by professional sports. This fundamental shift now permeates many campuses. Big-time college basketball and football have a professional look and feel—in their arenas and stadiums, their luxury boxes and financing, their uniforms and coaching staffs, and their marketing and administrative structures.[13]

Again the Commission locates the most acute problems in three areas: "academic transgressions, a financial arms race, and commercialization."[14] And again, the Commission suggests that placing power and control in the hand of university presidents will allow these problems to be addressed with the proper values at the fore.

The Commission's third report focuses largely on financial reforms. The emphasis is on tamping down on all kinds of athletic spending from limiting coaches' salaries, to curtailing TV contracts, to encouraging metrics that gauge the validity of athletic spending per student in relationship to spending per student in the university at large.[15] These limitations are

12. Several studies already mentioned provide clear statistical information indicating disadvantage. Harper et al., "Black Male Student-Athletes," and Staurowsky and Huma, *The Price of Poverty in Big-Time College Sports,* are two who paint a clear picture.

13. Knight Commission, *Call to Action,* 13.

14 Ibid.

15. When we talk about coaches' salaries we have to take into account a few important factors including the pressures for coaches to win and the tenuous way that coaches occupy space in university communities. Some can argue that big salaries are the market's consolation for the lack of job security, the ridiculous hours, and the unrelenting pressure to win. Inflated salaries are lifted up as a symptom of the problems with big-time sports—I would agree, but not for the reasons that many suggest. In a capitalist society, we assent to the way the market creates value. There are very few coaches (but I admit there are some and they are often the most sought after and most highly paid) who like the fact that coaches' lives are so deeply determined by wins and losses. Many coaches,

to come from increased transparency about athletic spending as well as from a redistribution of the spoils from conference and TV incomes that reward universities based on academic success instead of just winning.[16]

The Commission repeatedly described what is needed to solve problems in terms of limitation, control, and regulation of the out of control "alien" values of athletics. This framework of otherizing the world of sports gained traction and has largely defined the debate since. And the rhetoric, the problems solving strategies, and the institutions that have formed around academics and athletics echo with this theme. The main thrust of this otherizing is that revenue sports threaten the integrity of universities. And the best we can hope for is enforced conformity of the more laudable values of academic community. This conformity is a defense against the contaminating effect of things like commercialization, professionalism, cheating, and the relaxation of academic excellence.

An apocalyptic scrutiny of this framing of the epic conflict between athletics and academics, however, reveals an even more disturbing reality. The apocalypse reveals our distorted reality. We are told to assume that the threats to academic integrity come from athletics, but the threats are much more stealthy than that. Threats to the integrity of academic institutions are not from alien values infiltrating universities through athletic programs. The most devastating threats to the integrity of academic institutions come from the very assumptions that inform how we see and understand these problems.

---

however, care about their players and want to invest in them as people. Many coaches care about the universities they work for and want to invest in them as communities. But the patterns and paradigms of big-time sports create more energy around the next bigger and better thing. Coaches can never feel completely settled about their investment in a university, because they know that with a few losses their time there can be up and the university will bring in a new staff and start the cycle again. We had chances to leave UNC for NFL jobs and other college jobs, but we chose to stay because we really wanted to invest in the university and the players. We wanted to stay. Universities, and the systems of big-time sports in general, do not reward that kind of commitment and loyalty. And coaches are demonized when they choose to move on to the next big job. While we have tried to never let that be our driving force behind decisions, we understand the conditions that give rise to such fickle relationships between coaches and universities. A coach can stay and a university signals its commitment with dollars, but not with any promises of longevity or perseverance. No matter how highly coaches are paid, a university will not hesitate to terminate them if they don't win.

16. Knight Commission, *Restoring the Balance*, 14

POWER TOOLS

Privilege is . . . the ability to define reality for others, and to expect that definition to stick because you have the power to ensure that it becomes the dominant narrative.[17]

A primary indicator of this distorted logic reveals itself in the way power has been commonly exercised and encouraged. The Knight Commission's decision-making strategies at every turn embody a devastating lack of engagement with the people most affected by their recommendations—the young men and women who compete in Division I athletics and the coaches who work with them every day. While they indicate in each report their concern for the athletes themselves, the voices of currently enrolled athletes were never included in decision-making.[18] A historical roster of all the members of the Commission during its decades of service confirms that no athlete who was competing at the time ever served on the Commission as a voting member.[19] And no current coach has ever served on the Commission either.

The Knight Commission has never had an athlete currently competing in collegiate sports or a coach as a member.

This method of gathering in power is not unique to the Knight Commission. The deficit, however, is particularly troubling in this context because of the problems that the Commission was convened to address. Recall from the previous chapter that a mark of white culture is the formation of decision-making structures in which the people least affected by the decisions have the most power to make decisions. While the Knight Commission has no formal power in terms of enforcement, it has embodied a

17. Wise, *Speaking Treason Fluently*, 249.

18. Knight Commission reports describe things like surveys and hearings at a few junctures in the work of the Commission that engaged a variety of constituencies that included some players and some coaches.

19. In an email correspondence with Amy Perko, Executive Director of the Knight Commission, I was able to confirm that Knight Commission membership has not ever included a currently enrolled athlete. Ms. Perko shared that "In June 2008, the Commission added two former college athletes who had participated within the last five years of their appointment." Upon closer scrutiny, however, the one college football player who was named to the Commission in 2008, Christopher Zorich, graduated from Notre Dame in 1991 so had not played collegiate ball within five years of his tenure on the Commission. He also resigned after only two years on the Committee. She added, "Throughout its history, the Commission has invited current athletes to participate in various meetings." Email correspondence January 2, 1014.

uniquely privileged ability to define the problems on university campuses with sports for decades. While it may not have the ability to legislate or enforce its recommendations, it certainly has had an impact defining paradigms that people and institutions use to understand the problem of big-time sports on college campuses. The NCAA directly adopted many of the Commission's recommendations. While many of these initiatives did not produce much of the desired impact, the Commission has continued to have a potent position in framing the issues for universities and for the NCAA. The Commission has defined problems and encouraged solutions without the voices and votes of current players or coaches in the particular sports that they pinpoint as at the heart of the problems they address. And the Knight Commission is largely composed of both current and past presidents of several of the universities that have big-time sports themselves.[20]

From its most basic strategy of developing understanding and addressing problems, the Knight Commission has been distorted by privilege and white mentalities. This often unconscious exercise of privilege around an issue in which the majority of the participants in the context under scrutiny are people of color creates conditions ripe for persistent yet camouflaged racialized disadvantage. This particular kind of camouflage plays tricks on us all, even on the disadvantaged themselves. The potent rhetoric both of institutions of higher learning and of the world of big-time sports creates the appearance of promise and a chance to succeed. This camouflage shimmers of inclusion in a community of learning and growth, and of better access to opportunities. This camouflage is also made more attractive by the perceived chance to play professionally beyond college that playing Division I ball can make possible.[21]

This camouflage is even more effective than something that just dazzles the disadvantaged into assenting to participation in an activity that does not have the payoffs that it boasts. This camouflage passes muster for the privileged because it cloaks disadvantage in the appearance of

20. UNC President Emeritus Dr. Bill Friday was one of the co-chairs of the Knight Commission for years. At a community forum in 2012 at UNC during the football scandal, Dr. Friday and Taylor Branch were two of the respondents. My husband, John, asked Dr. Friday what UNC could have done to better advocate for the young men who were wrongly accused in the football investigation. Dr. Friday responded with a confused expression and said, "I am not aware of anything that wasn't provided for them."

21. Most recent statistics tell us that between 1.8 percent of Division I football players will go on to play in the NFL and 1.2 percent of Division I basketball players will go on to play in the NBA. Harper and Quaye, eds., *Student Engagement in Higher Education*, 141.

appropriate avenues of opportunity for racial minorities. In other words, the fact that sports is an avenue toward respectability, opportunity, and success for people of color resonates with white mentalities. It easily follows the pathways of unexpressed and sometimes unconscious prejudices secretly held by whites that people of color are not capable of "making it" the same way white people do.

The narrative around academics and athletics broadcast by the Knight Commission resonates with those in power. And these same narratives around big-time sports resonate with those who seek opportunity and seek access to power in a culture where this route is accepted, recognized, and encouraged. In an effective symbiotic relationship the Knight Commission has worked with the NCAA to try and create "change." This clarion call to change has reverberated with privilege. The change these entities seek is to squash nonconformity to their established ideals. These entities seek an end to the dangerous boundary crossing they attribute to renegade athletic programs in university settings that are becoming too important.

The history of the NCAA and its methods of garnering power and influence embodies many of the troubling dynamics inherent in the white lines people in power like to maintain. Marks of paternalism and privilege have had a deeply formative effect when we consider the structure and dynamics of the NCAA. And the NCAA functions and exerts influence purely through the consent of institutions of higher learning. Many people do not realize that it is the member institutions of the NCAA that decide on and mete out punishment on their athletes and their athletic program, not the NCAA itself. The NCAA enforces its huge rulebook mostly through a mythical power structure of accountability propped up by intimidation and threats of utter destruction to programs that do not comply. Compliance is enforced from within the member institutions themselves for fear of getting on the wrong side of NCAA investigators. These elusive structures of enforcement and punishment are veiled in secrecy. Institutions are told not to discuss investigations or they will be punished. Institutions are told to cooperate or their non-cooperation will be "interpreted as unethical behavior."[22] Institutions are told to come up with their own sanctions in hopes that

> *It is the university that rules a player ineligible, not the NCAA. The NCAA advises and recommends, but the member institutions determine the status of their athletes.*

22. Branch, "Shame of College Sports," 15.

those self-imposed sanctions will satisfy the NCAA and prevent further reprisals.[23] As mentioned in the previous chapter, the sizeable NCAA manual has nothing to say about the rights of the athlete. The status of the athlete hinges totally on the system of eligibility created by the NCAA that has no due process for athletes accused of violations.

Both the Knight Commission and the NCAA lean heavily on an emotional, visceral reaction that many people (and many of them people with power in institutions of higher learning) have about athletes being paid for their labor or receiving "unfair" advantage from their status as an athlete. The elusive sacred cow of amateurism (which has no legal definition) and the moniker of "student-athlete" (coined by the NCAA in order to sidestep a workers comp case) provide the shaky ground for the core principals we are collectively told we need to protect as "cherished" and "precious."[24] This apocalypse unveils a troubling subtext: athletes need to stay in their place and not get overzealous about their place in the community. And the NCAA creates the mechanism for universities to do that with no input from the athletes themselves.

Apocalypse reveals the real offense. The offense is not athletes overstepping their bounds. *The offense is the subtly repeated insistence of white power brokers that athletes are invasive, alien, corrupting interlopers who need to be controlled. These caricatures thrive when there is little to no cultivation of substantive relationships between the stakeholders.* Rather than encouraging connection, collaboration, and relationship, as we would expect in communities of higher learning, these patterns of enforcement and penalty have further segregated the people who need to connect with each other the most.

In a bitter twist of institutionalized irony, the principles that are called on to help athletes "blend in" with the rest of the student body and not have special status have authorized a distorted singling out of players in

23. The University of Minnesota pushed back against the NCAA when it decided not to assent to their demands. The University of Miami and Penn State are two examples of institutions that also decided to push back when the NCAA exacted further sanctions and monetary punishment in the wake of investigations. Penn State has pending litigation around the monetary penalties. The University of Miami effectively called the NCAA's bluff when it encouraged tougher sanctions and the NCAA backed down. Auburn University's refusal to sit Cam Newton is another example. To save face, the NCAA uncharacteristically ruled in lighting speed that Newton was cleared of any wrongdoing and could play. The NCAA is a nonprofit entity that arguably has no legal grounds for its enforcement of its member institutions.

24. Branch, "Shame of College Sports," 9, 26, 27.

Division I revenue sports.[25] These players, who are generating millions of dollars through their play, are put into a singular bind characterized by three troubling realities:

- Athletes are unable to benefit from their play beyond their scholarships. These scholarships, however, leave the vast majority of those players who compete in the revenue sports (football and men's basketball) living well under the federal poverty line and with some of the lowest graduation rates in the country.[26] Players help generate billions but some cannot afford to buy a suit for a job interview when their playing days are over, or even buy food while they are under scholarship.

- Athletes are compelled (unknowingly) to sign away basic human rights in order to play. On national signing day rights like due process are signed away in the National Letter of Intent (NLI). This provision and the "daily operations" of the NLI are managed by the NCAA, which puts the athlete under the jurisdiction of the NCAA rulebook. Not one page of the NCAA rulebook addresses the rights of student athletes.[27]

- Once enrolled and eligible for play, athletes are cajoled into compliance with the threat of losing the "privilege" to play Division I college sports because of rules violations based on staying eligible—a status determined by universities in consultation with the NCAA. The need to stay eligible has created a culture of institutional habits for maintaining eligibility that sometimes do not support substantive learning and academic growth. The massive NCAA rule book is used to limit everything from meals eaten off campus, to rides to the airport, to fair wages for work unrelated to sports, to what kinds of tutoring and mentoring an athlete can receive.

This singular bind creates constrained spaces for relationships to develop, for study to be robust, and for complicated situations to be acknowledged and addressed. Athletes occupy space in learning communities that do not encourage the same kinds of growth and experience that other students

25. Knight Commission, *Call to Action*, 26.

26. Staurowsky and Huma's study (*The Price of Poverty in Bigtime College Sports*) gives us unequivocal evidence that "full scholarships" do not provide a livable situation for the majority of college athletes.

27. For information on the National Letter of Intent, see http://www.nationalletter. org/index.html.

occupy. Many of these constraints emerge from the stated intentions of entities like the NCAA, the Knight Commission, and the universities themselves to prevent any advantage an athlete may gain from his/her status as an athlete. This bind literally cuts off healthy patterns of circulation in communities of higher learning for everyone.

IMMERSION LEARNING

> I learned the most in the Carolina community through the difficult and invisible work of relationship building.[28]

While at UNC we encountered several places where these habits of mind and segregating policies diminished the health of the university. After John was fired along with all the other coaches, we stayed in Chapel Hill for an additional year to continue to seek change and advocate for the athletes John had made promises to when he recruited them to UNC. Many of the faculty members who reached out to us during this time voiced feelings of disconnection from players. And players voiced similar feelings about faculty. Both cited feelings of intimidation about seeking out conversations with the other. One UNC official in the athletic department told John that it was the players' responsibility to cultivate relationships with their professors. When John suggested that professors also had a responsibility to cultivate those relationships and actually had more power to do so, the official confessed never having looked at it from that perspective. One UNC faculty member who had taken an interest in building such relationships with football players told us that athletic officials had told him to "back off" because he was getting "too close" to the players.[29]

During John's tenure as a coach at UNC he invited numerous faculty members and administrators to come and sit in his football meeting room to get to know the players better and hear what they talked about in his meeting room. No one ever took him up on his offer. One professor told him that it was much too intimidating for him to walk into the football office. When John suggested that players probably feel that way about academic buildings, the professor said he had never considered that perspective. UNC, despite its identity as a learning community for diverse

28. Shoop, "Thanks, Amazing Student Athletes."

29. Studies show that faculty in American universities tend to spend more time with white students than they do with black students. Harper, Williams, and Blackman, "Black Male Student-Athletes and Racial Inequities," 6.

populations, did not cultivate the kind of boundary crossing that diverse communities need in order for substantive relationships to develop and flourish. And the specter of NCAA violations weaves its way through these constrained and blocked spaces in ways that further entrenches caution, distrust, and fear when it comes to building relationships across cultures.

We attended, with select faculty and players, a lunch meeting with *New York Times* reporter Joe Nocera, who was invited to campus because of his story on UNC player Devon Ramsay. We were astounded to witness how much shared understanding and substantive conversation developed during just one lunch between the faculty and the players. The professors all remarked that they had never heard the perspectives the players shared. To a person they said that these perspectives changed their understanding of the situation. We all lamented that such space had not been cleared for these conversations before. If it had, I venture to say things at UNC could have been drastically different.

THE SCIENCE OF DISADVANTAGE

> Perhaps more outrage and calls for accountability would ensue if there were greater awareness of the actual extent to which college sports persistently disadvantage Black male student-athletes.[30]

The NCAA is the ultimate bully when it comes to keeping this dysfunctional system intact. It creates and maintains an unjust system and then uses punishment of those it is exploiting as its most potent check on aberrant behavior. And many of the institutions that admit the players and benefit from their hard work do little (if anything) to protect these members of their community from the vagaries of NCAA accusations and sanctions.[31] Division I football and basketball athletes, amidst all the laments about their special status, occupy a space that is characterized by a unique kind of disadvantage.

It is here, at this unique and distorted space of disadvantage, that the lifted veil has the most to show us. If we are interested in truly changing the most harmful aspects of revenue sports intermingled with institutions of

---

30. Ibid., 1.

31. There are some schools that are better than others at advocating for players. Often heightened advocacy seems to be connected to the most lucrative programs (SEC football schools, for instance, are known as schools that tend to protect their players against NCAA sanctions). One could chalk this up to the hypothesis that programs with more to lose financially from losing key players from their championship teams do more to protect their investments.

higher learning, we must engage this space of disadvantage. And this space of disadvantage has been mistaken for a space of advantage—rendering our need to gaze at it from a different perspective a difficult stretch and strain for many people. Are we ready for the scaffolding that has supported our collective interpretations of these problems to be dismantled?

For many, it may feel like there is a lot to lose in that dismantling. What many stand to lose is their ability to maintain their own space of advantage—a space they did not perceive as advantage but instead understood as responsible, enlightened, and correct. The Knight Commission and the NCAA are not the protectors of what we hold most dear on American campuses. On the contrary, they have helped to prop up a tenacious set of illusions that have done harm to some of the most life-giving aspirations of higher education. If academic communities aspire to be true learning communities where every one experiences life-enhancing growth and transformation, then relationships must be built from real lives and not from distorted caricatures and stereotypes.

The fact is that studies and statistics do not back up a lot of how the problems of revenue sports on college campuses have been depicted. Academic improprieties, cheating, dummy classes, loosened admission standards are all places of concern, but not problems unique to sports. Studies of cheating rates in fact tell us something very different. The disturbing reality is that most students cheat: 75 to 98 percent of college students today say they cheated on academic work during high school. And some of the worst offenders are the best students, who have the most to lose when it comes to grades. One poll found that 80 percent of top students admit cheating to get to the top of their class.[32] The prevalence of cheating is deeply disturbing. Revenue sports are not the culprit.[33]

32. Cheating rates among athletes is no higher than it is among the larger student body. Statistics even suggest that rates among athletes are better than the rates for the general student body. One resource for cheating statistics describes the "profile of college students more likely to cheat: Business or Engineering majors; Those whose future plans include business; Men self-report cheating more than woman; Fraternity and Sorority members; Younger students; Students with lower GPAs or those at the very top." See http://www.glass-castle.com/clients/www-nocheating-org/adcouncil/research/cheating-factsheet.html.

Still another study listed percentages by occupation of those who feel cheating is necessary to get ahead. Sports and athletics did not even make the list. See http://josephsoninstitute.org/surveys/.

33. Still other ills on college campuses like alcohol abuse and sexual violence are often associated with athletes who are described as being above the rules. Statistics tell us that

Dummy classes and loosened admission standards are also red herrings. While anyone interested in academic integrity will agree that classes that don't actually meet and classes that don't require any work should not be a part of one's academic experience, most people answer a jovial "yes" to the question of whether they had any "bunny courses" in college.

> *75 to 98 percent of college students say they cheated on academic work during high school.*

The more pressing question is about the quality of education players are encouraged to receive during their tenure as a student. If players should be thankful "just to have a scholarship" as many people remark when the question of paying players comes up, shouldn't that scholarship mean they get a life-enhancing education? While NCAA and university standards about eligibility had the desire for players to receive a "meaningful degree" as their stated intention, the effect of these regulations has often taken things in the opposite direction. The stakes are so high for coaches (losing games raises the threat of being fired) and players (being ineligible means running the risk of losing one's scholarship and one's chance to play professionally) and universities (lucrative big-time sports programs help pay the bills and keep powerful alumni happy) when it comes to winning games, that working to stay eligible can too often replace life-giving learning.[34] This deficit

---

these problems are most pronounced among other groups on campus, especially within the Greek system of fraternities and sororities. Some stats for sexual assault, for instance, tell us that 55 percent of gang rapes are by fraternities, while 40 percent are by sports teams. See http://www.oneinfourusa.org/statistics.php. While both are sobering numbers, this problem is not endemic to sports itself, but perhaps to other more entrenched dynamics on campus particularly around the abuse of alcohol. Seventy thousand sexual assaults on campus a year are connected to the abuse of alcohol. "Fraternities and sororities are among the key groups that foster this culture of drinking on campus. Their members drink far greater amounts of alcohol, and do so more frequently than other members, setting a norm for heavy drinking. A national study on college drinking found that fraternity members were much more likely to engage in heavy drinking than their non-fraternity peers. Approximately 50 percent of students living in a fraternity or sorority house performed poorly on a test or project, versus about 25 percent of all students. Eighty-three percent of residents in a fraternity or sorority house experienced negative consequences due to other students' drinking, such as a serious argument, assault, property damage, having to take care of a drunken student, interrupted sleep or study, an unwanted sexual advance, or sexual assault or acquaintance rape." Higher Education Center for Alcohol and Other Drug Abuse and Violence Prevention, "Fraternity and Sorority Members and Alcohol and Other Drug Use," para. 2.

34. UNC staff member Mary Willingham has been vocal about her findings that some athletes at UNC could not read. UNC officials have questioned her data, and she has even received death threats for voicing her concerns. Ganim, "UNC Whistle-Blower

in a player's learning is not always the case. And it is dangerous to assume that football and basketball players are all bogus students. Many are hardworking students with healthy amounts of academic curiosity and drive. Eligibility can work against these students, too, as academic support staff can sometimes steer them toward classes that they have the resources to help them with through the university tutors. Devon Ramsay, for instance, was discouraged from enrolling in an upper level economics class by academic support staff who told him they did not have any tutoring to provide for upper level economics classes.

Admissions standards provide another window into some collectively held and often unconscious assumptions. Individual universities have their own systems and formulae for admission, but the alarm about athletes getting special dispensation ignores the processes in place through which *all* admission decisions are made. There are many things that admission officers take into account in their decisions, including things that have nothing to do with academic achievement. Some of these factors include participation in extracurricular activities, travel, demonstrated leadership, unique experiences and abilities (including artistic, musical, and technological), family members who have attended that institution (legacy admission), and other intangibles like what a person brings to the community that others may not.

If we bring athletic ability alongside these other factors, it may not seem so alarming that these particular skills and talents are taken into account. *Is there some particular kind of offense when a young black male gets into a school, not simply based on his football playing ability but with that talent taken into account? Do our standards of academic integrity suffer the same offense when a university admits a student who is an amazing violin player but who may not have scored as high as others on his/her math SAT?* How does it sit with us collectively to hear that "primary legacies," or those who had a parent attend an institution in some of the most selective universities of the country, can enjoy a very pronounced advantage in admission? In some cases legacies are as much as 45 percent more likely to be admitted than non-legacies.[35]

Battles for OK."

35. "In other words, if a non-legacy applicant faced a 15-percent chance of admission, an identical applicant who was a primary legacy would have a 60-percent chance of getting in." Ashburn, "At Elite Colleges, Legacy Status May Count," para. 3.

The problem is not the professionalization or commercialization when it comes to sports either. Universities don't push back against these dynamics in other programs—the Business school, the Law School, the Medical School, or programs for the Arts. Professionalization is not routinely cast as a problem in other guilds that receive training in institutions of higher learning. Sports are placed in a different category despite the fact that it is a fully professionalized phenomenon in our capitalist society. Even though many universities have graduate programs in things like sports management, they still push back against acknowledging the athletes, the reason sports are so popular and lucrative in our culture, as legitimate practitioners of a professional skill when they are laboring at their craft. Our society is so repulsed by this possibility that there widespread support for classifying any contact from sports agents to collegiate players as a felony offense.

Under closer scrutiny the issue of concern here is not that academic standards are malleable in their capacity to fit different contexts or that there is professionalization on college campuses. This concern is more likely linked to some tenaciously unconscious assumptions that many in academia hold deep inside of them. These assumptions are fed by something more offensive than malleable admission standards. These deep unconscious assumptions need to be surfaced. These assumptions have more to do with race and privilege than they have to do with academic integrity and ethics. These assumptions are formed and fed by generations of unexamined privilege and by communities sequestered by racialized experiences—and I include whiteness in that category of racialized. *Unconscious racialized assumptions will continue to distort our collective vision until these cataracts of privilege are diagnosed and removed.*

The apocalypse when it comes to academic communities and big-time sports certainly reveals a crisis of integrity. The fault line that reveals itself has to do with power, equity, and even good old-fashioned fairness. The closer I get to how universities with revenue producing sports and the NCAA operate, the clearer things come into focus. The challenges to academic integrity come from many places including pressure to succeed, alcohol abuse, grade inflation, and the banality of dishonesty among human beings. Sports come alongside these common character traits on American college campuses and add to the mix, but perhaps not even remarkably so.

Graduation rates, for instance, used to measure the academic integrity of athletic programs, reveal a lower rate of graduation for black male athletes. Graduation rates for black male athletes on campuses with big-time football programs are often startling lower than the graduation rates of the overall student body. But when the graduation rates of black athletes are compared to those of black males in the overall student body, the differentials are not as pronounced. These statistics beg the question: why are university campuses not more successful at graduating their black male students overall? And why have we focused on athletic programs as the problem area when the rates show a deficit in the overall graduation rates for black male students?[36] And do we have the eyes to see how the very systems set up to keep athletes' status as legitimate students have diminished their chances to receive a life-enhancing education?

The rupture in integrity comes in the hypocrisy of the lofty rhetoric that most institutions of higher learning boast about their values around equity, diversity, and learning community that ring hollow through the vast architecture of big-time sports. This architecture was built and is maintained on the backs of an unpaid and exploited work force. And the lifted veil shows us the stark reality—that unpaid and exploited work force is composed largely of young men of color who are working in conditions that create more disadvantage than advantage. And despite the clarity of this picture from many sources, the societal rhetoric among college presidents and athletic directors all over the country continues to be about the battle between the false foes of academics and athletics.

What if the framework shifted away from the emphasis on making academic standards for athletes higher and higher, toward creating the conditions necessary for community-wide integrity to emerge? Integrity can only emerge when difficult and substantive questions are asked about how power is exercised and shared. True learning communities centered on life-enhancing education for all can't abide by statistical realties like the achievement gap, like racialized disadvantage, like certain groups of people being denied basic human rights such as due process. Cultivating the conditions necessary for community-wide integrity is not about coddling athletes so they can remain eligible—it is about justice, fairness, and equity. These terms sound so very American, so very facile to our democratic ears. Yet we Americans are hard of hearing when it comes to the testimonies of the long-term deficits created by slavery and racism in all of our systems of merit and achievement.

36 Harper, Williams, and Blackman, "Black Male Student-Athletes and Racial Inequities."

Can universities take a look at the marks of privilege and elitism that have helped to create, obscure, and authorize systems of injustice and inequity? It depends on how those with the power to change the conversation frame the problems and the solutions. The uneasy relationship between athletics and academics calls out for these demons to be exorcised. We must be able to name these demons without fear. *Things must change in the world of big-time sports in order for institutions of higher learning to have the integrity they aspire to have in their communities.* The stakes are higher than the millions, even billions, of dollars that course through the veins of universities because of big-time sports. *At stake is the very nature of education and growth that universities give its students, indeed all of the members of their communities.* For our collective learning to elevate us all out of the distortions that big-time sports currently embody, we must dig into the very roots of what forms our communities and our communal aspirations. These basic building blocks of human life are informed by the nature of the connections we cultivate with each other.

BACK TO BASICS

When John and I learned about the NCAA investigation at UNC I remember the sinking feeling we had about what it could mean for us. After Coach Butch Davis called John to let him know what was happening, a quick trip around the Internet for me was enough to create a terrible sense of foreboding. In the months and even years that followed as the investigation played out, we realized in sometimes excruciating moments that the investigation was going to change our lives forever. It has done that, but not in ways that we expected or feared in the beginning of it all. At the beginning, we felt angry at and betrayed by the people accused of wrongdoing. It felt like a terrible breach of trust and lapse of judgment. From what we could gather the transgressions centered around two things. First, there were three players who attended a party in Miami hosted by a sports agent, which was an NCAA violation. Second, one of John's colleagues, Coach John Blake, was suspected of having a potentially problematic relationship with an agent that the NCAA alleged affected his relationships with players.

Our first reactions centered on being wronged by these people we had trusted. This feeling of betrayal is a well-worn pattern of reaction in the football business. It is hard to trust people in this profession, which John often says can feel like a game of *Survivor*. So we positioned ourselves for the first several months of the investigation alongside the university and its efforts to absolutely comply with the demands of the NCAA. Like fearful children, coaches, players, and athletic administrators sought ways to get back into the good graces of the angry grownups—the NCAA, media outlets reporting on the investigation, and university administrators.

With each player who was added to the list of accused—which quickly went from three to thirteen and finally to eighteen by the end of the investigation—we felt more and more victimized ourselves. This feeling of being wronged was troubled early on by the fact that all the players accused were black, as was the only coach accused of wrongdoing. While the racial divide bothered us, we did little to question it beyond our own private conversations about our discomfort with that fact. Most of our energy centered on how our lives were becoming more and more difficult to navigate because of the investigation. How were the coaches supposed to do their jobs with so many players held out of games? Why were those of us who did nothing wrong being punished for the suspected transgressions of others?

John and his colleagues hunkered down and vowed to do their jobs well in the midst of it all. They modeled for the players tuning out distractions and taking care of your responsibilities in ways that best helped the team. The athletic and university administration instructed coaches and players not to talk about the investigation with anyone. This gag order coupled with the rigors of a normal football season allowed John and me to maintain what we would later realize was a distorted posture toward what was happening at UNC. It was not until the University changed course and fired head coach Butch Davis just days before the 2011 season was to begin that we began to speak out.

I am embarrassed to admit that it took realizing that we were effectively exiled from the UNC community ourselves for us to substantively speak out about and act on the distortions that the investigation was revealing. When a head coach is fired, the writing is routinely on the wall for all the assistant coaches that they, too, will be terminated. UNC simply played this dynamic out in slow motion by firing Coach Davis before the season started and retaining the rest of the coaching staff until the season was over. Our casting out was an excruciating time lapse of realizations, grief, anger, and transformation. What emerged during this time lapse included profound questions around how players are treated in college sports in general and deeply troubling realizations about the culture of UNC in particular. Our greatest teachers were the players themselves, especially those who lost the most. When I started writing my "Calling Audibles" blog series more teachers emerged—parents of players, faculty, people who love sports and care about justice, alumni who were grieving the actions of their *alma mater*, reporters, activists, and other coaches and people who have been involved with sports for a long time.[37]

We were brought back to the thing that has always mattered to us the most in our life in sports—relationships, the most basic building block of being a team and being a community. And we learned anew that it was at this most basic layer of what makes sports life-giving that was being distorted and contorted in Division I revenue sports. This distortion may sound obvious and even trite, but this distortion and the illusions it spawns have a tenacious hold on all of us who intersect with the sports world. Some of us are more diminished by these distortions than others, but all of us are less than what we can be because of their power.

The apocalypse when it comes to higher learning and big-time sports may tell us more about what it means to be white in this country than it tells us about academic integrity. The NCAA scandal at UNC provided my family and me with an exposure to these realities, which has changed the character of how we understand our vocations and ourselves. The dynamics of big-time sports on university campuses conspires against life-giving and lasting relationships, relationships that make communities and the world we live in better.

The university's own commitment to being an institution that "with *lux, libertas*—light and liberty—as its founding principles . . . chart[s] a bold course of leading change to improve society and to help solve the world's greatest problems" was fundamentally violated by institutional practices used in the football investigation.[38] The university states that part of its mission is to "teach a diverse community of students . . . to become the next generation of leaders." Far from cultivating the skills needed for leadership in a diverse and global world, the university's problem-solving strategies embodied a deep ambivalence toward the realities of life in diverse communities. Sharing power, listening to voices other than the voices of those who hold institutional power, making space for justice that takes into account the complexities of big-time football, and just simply having in place standards of due process, were never on the table as institutional

37. Mount Shoop, *Calling Audibles*, www.marciamountshoop.com.

38. For the full mission statement of the University of North Carolina, see http://www.unc.edu/ugradbulletin/mission.html.

concerns. Until these demons that afflict institutions of higher learning are called by name, they will continue their relentless pursuit of conflict and diminished returns. And higher learning will remain a rhetorical aspiration rather than a live option for us all.

7

Touchdowns for Jesus[1]

Tell John Kasay that God doesn't care about football.
She's a baseball fan.

THE 1998 SEASON HAD been rough so far for the NFL Carolina Panthers. We had lost five games in a row to start the season. The game
against Tampa Bay was a big one. Everyone was feeling the pressure. We
really needed a win. Our very dependable kicker, John Kasay, who had hit
multiple field goals to keep us firmly in the game, missed one that would
have tied it up in the last few seconds to put the game into overtime. When
asked about the missed kick in a post-game press conference, Kasay said

---

1. This chapter contains portions of a post in my *Calling Audibles* blog series. The
post, by the same name as this chapter, was written in response to the explosion of media
attention given to Tim Tebow when he was playing for the Denver Broncos during the
2011 NFL season. "Tebowing" was the focus of much scrutiny. When the Broncos started
winning some games with nothing short of miraculous comebacks, people started to
wonder if Tebowing was actually having an effect on the outcomes of games. When the
Broncos ran out of magic in the playoffs, the theological complexity became too much
for the hyped-up conversation. And just when the conversation was getting interesting
it died down and Tebow got cut from the team. Tebow is not the first player to elicit
such a response in the media. A similar dynamic occurred with the Detroit Lions in the
2007 season when Jon Kitna was quarterback, as described in Krattenmaker, *Onward
Christian Athletes*, 69–76. Most sports fan can probably think of several other examples
as well.

that the wind had suddenly changed and that God must not have wanted the Panthers to win that day.

A minister friend of mine, of the progressive Christian persuasion, asked me to deliver his witty retort to Kasay's comment: "God doesn't care about football, she's a baseball fan." His message, delivered with a smile, is loaded with theological suggestion. And the line it walks is where many Christians teeter around the question of how God takes up space in the sports we love. My minister friend's answer came loaded with his own theological rebuttal. In one turn of phrase he deconstructed Kasay's assumptions about the character of God and replaced them with enough humor to leave the question of how God's power intersects with sports still a lingering curiosity.

The Panthers continued to struggle that season with seemingly countless injuries and losses in close games. Despite the team owner's promise mid-season that he was behind the coaching staff 100 percent (the dreaded vote of confidence), the coaching staff was fired at the end of the season. While Kasay's theological assumptions sometimes did not resonate with our own about how God was at work in that season, we certainly did feel God's providential hand at work in the midst of it all. After all, it is things like missed field goals, fumbles, and fickle owners that can change the course of our family's life in profound ways.

After the Panthers dismissed the coaches, John and I moved to Chicago for him to take a job with the Bears. In Chicago I received my first call to the ministry and our son was born. Our years in Chicago were full of God's grace-filled presence in the midst of the in and outs and ups and downs of football. We inhabited communities of people who helped to shape our lives in more ways than we can count. Surely God's hand was in it all. And that errant field goal was a part of what set it all into motion.

As a pastor and theologian, people often ask me if it is okay to pray for wins. I say, "Sure, as long as you're praying for the same team I am." All kidding aside, I confess that I do pray during football games. On my best days, I am praying for peace, for calm, for good things to unfold. I am praying for the players and the coaches. I am praying for everyone to enjoy, to do their best, and to be safe from injury. I admit that in desperate times and in the heat of the moment, I have prayed for things like touchdowns and wins. Who hasn't uttered prayers that are theologically inconsistent when the going gets rough? Even with my occasional red-zone prayers, I do not believe that God is the great fixer of football games in the sky. It should go without saying that if God worked in such a mechanistic, puppeteer-like way that God engineered wins and losses then we would not have hungry children with distended bellies in the world, or war, or children who are abused by the adults who are supposed to take care of them.

Where does God's love and care start and stop in the world of big-time sports? How do we parse out divine presence, transcendence, Holy Mystery in the midst of first downs, unlikely catches, big tackles, and upset wins? How we answer these questions is no incidental matter. These answers reflect our assumptions about divine power, about human responsibility, and about how we live with life's pain and promise. An unveiling of the intersections of Christianity and big-time sports reveals distortions in places we might not expect. *The ways we allow each other and ourselves to scrutinize what the apocalypse reveals tells us a lot about the communities we long for and about the communities we actually inhabit.*

PIETY AND PIGSKIN

John spent twelve years coaching in the NFL on four different teams. We saw situations where team chemistry was strengthened by faith and we saw situations where team chemistry was fractured by faith. In the places where it seemed to divide, faith fed an ethos of exclusion and judgment. With almost 100 players on a football team at different parts of the season, the law of averages tells us that there are people of diverse faiths on every team. There is a chilling effect on people being "out" about their faith when one way of believing is held up as the only right way.

On some of these teams it was not just people of other faiths who were marginalized. Christians who didn't conform to a particular way of understanding and expressing their faith were alienated, too. Coaches' Bible studies and pregame chapel services were some of the places where the abiding intolerance was expressed. I was even kicked out of a coaches' wives' Bible study on one team because I suggested we could study more than one interpretation of scripture. And even though I am an ordained minister who has preached and lectured in all kinds of churches all over the country, I have never been asked to speak at a team chapel service in John's twenty-two-plus years of coaching. This exclusion may well have something to do with my gender in addition to my "brand" of Christianity; after all, these two aspects of who I am as a Christian are not disconnected.

In the places where faith seemed to strengthen the teams we were a part of, it enhanced everyone's ability to connect, to persevere, to put things in perspective, and to kindle generosity and compassion for one another. Those were places where there was room for nonconformity to one way of believing. Those were places with space for more robust faith conversations. And when there was a misstep and people felt marginalized or offended, they voiced those feelings and people learned from it. In the NFL, however, it was a more common dynamic for Christianity to conform to the familiar template that we see in big-time sports.

You do not have to be on the inside of big-time sports to recognize this template of Christian expression. Big-time athletes who express their faith in ways like thanking Jesus Christ for a win, pointing to the heavens after a big play, praying at the center of the field after games, and kneeling in the end zone after a touchdown are

> *The FCA was founded in 1954 to encourage athletes and coaches to endorse a Christian lifestyle.*

familiar images to any sports fan. This familiar template is not accidental. It is the result of the years of hard work and relationship building that groups like the FCA (Fellowship of Christian Athletes) and AIA (Athletes in Action) have done in the world of sports.[2] Their impact has been remarkable. When it comes to setting the tone for how Christianity and big-time sports connect, they are pretty much the only game in town.

AIA places over half of the team chaplains in the NFL.[3] The FCA was built on a model of capitalizing on the popularity of sports in order to bring more people to Christ. Its capacity to network and make connections with athletes from high school through the professional ranks is unrivaled. And it has built these relationships through some of the strong bonds that already exist in sports—the relationships between coaches and players. "The most effective way to reach more athletes, the FCA realized, is to first reach the coach."[4] And they have seized on the marketing power of star athletes that companies use to promote products. "If athletes can endorse shaving cream, razor blades, and cigarettes, surely they can endorse the Lord."[5] FCA and AIA have provided countless hours of Bible study, support, and teach-

2. Seward, "60 Years and Counting," 18.

3. Krattenmaker, *Onward Christian Athletes*, 18.

4. Seward, "60 Years and Counting," 20.

5. One of FCA's founders, Coach Don McClanen, said this to Dr. Louis Evans in order to share his vision of what the FCA could be. Ibid., 18.

ing for coaches and athletes. And they have guided athletes on how to witness to Christ through their athletic pursuits.

The distinctiveness of the influence of groups like FCA has also helped to shape the reaction others have to this common expression of Christianity in big-time sports. Some Christians react against the common ways that Christianity is expressed in big-time sports by trying to draw distinctions between sports and God's activity in the world. They

> *Early American Puritans brought with them from England a disdain for sports—they were seen as dangerous and trivial pastimes for Christians.*

push back at the belief that God decides whether field goals are good or not by asserting that these trivial matters are beneath God; Jesus doesn't care about football. The theological ramifications of this belief are profound.

If Jesus doesn't care about football, our love of sports becomes at best a guilty pleasure and at worst a sinful waste of time. This dismissal of sports as unworthy of God's attention echoes the suspicion that Puritans had toward sports early in America's religious history.[6] God stands apart from this trivial and overly important part of human life. This "I don't care about football" attitude, however, does not sound like the same Jesus who took his powerful love all the way into the bowels of hell to liberate the captives. It doesn't fit that Jesus would not care about something that captures our attention so acutely. Jesus' ministry was much more skillful than that. He moved about in the world with an utter immediacy to who and what was in front of him. I believe that if Jesus were here today in his ministry on this planet, he would make it his business to be well acquainted with something that holds our attention and elicits our passion that way big-time sports do. *I have a feeling that Jesus would be able to inhabit football stadiums much like he would inhabit modern day churches—with compassion, with hard truth, with an offer of healing, and with some parabolic wisdom that would knock your socks off.*

At either end of this theological continuum that stretches between these dissonant beliefs about God's connection to sports, there rests theological conclusions that threaten the very heart of the Christian

> *The demonic trivializes and diminishes divinity by making the universe all about us.*

witness. At one end we have the mechanistic God who controls our every move. This assumption about divine power gets us to an untenable deity:

6. Hoffman, *Good Game*, 86.

a God who lets children starve to death but conjures up a game changing wind just in time for the "right" team to win. And on the other end of this continuum we get a God who could not care less about the ins and outs of a football game. We end up with a deity that offends the core character of the covenantal God who Christians follow. At this extreme we get a God who recedes from loving us, caring for us, calling us to be who we were made to be simply because of a particular activity in which we are engaged. Both are distortions. Both exercise the demons of our tendency not to understand our place in the scheme of things. The apocalypse reveals that they are both about power—God's power and ours.

POWER PLAY

> How can we distinguish good power, the power of life, from evil power, the power to dominate? . . . The most important criterion for answering it is that good power is shared power, power which distributes itself, which involves others, which grows through dispersion and does not become less. In this sense the resurrection of Christ is a tremendous distribution of power.[7]

What is the nature of God's power? There are many different ways to answer this question. But no matter the flavor of the answer, one thing should hold true across the board: *God's power is unique.* It is not the same as the power that we humans have at our disposal. And as much as humans are prone to overlay the kinds of power we know onto God (e.g., dominance, might, force, control, etc.) to signal divine strength and potency, the way God operates in human life is singular and, in the end, mysterious. As Christians we get lots of clues about the nature of divine power through Christ, through the biblical witness, and through our own experience of God's presence in the world. Some of these clues tell us that *divine power is relational, it is loving, it is creative, and it is life-giving.*

The issue of power permeates the college game when it comes to how faith takes up space on sports teams. In college these issues morph from how we feel when celebrity players express strong beliefs on a gigantic stage into the ethics of how faith is navigated in settings in which there are pronounced power differentials between the people involved. As upsetting as some of the expressions of faith John and I encountered in the NFL were

7. Sölle, *Thinking about God*, 188.

(like when I got kicked out of the wives' Bible study for expressing a different interpretation of scripture), the abuses of power that we've experienced in the college game are much more problematic.

In college football, like the NFL, there are some prevalent streams of Christianity that course through most teams. These particular ways of interpreting and embodying the Christian faith, while they are not the way I generally choose to express my faith, are not problematic in and of themselves. They become problematic, however, when people with more power than the players (e.g., coaches or other staff members in football programs and athletic departments) endorse that particular expression of Christianity and put pressure on the players to adopt it as their own.

> *Abuse of power is the misuse of one's ability to direct or influence the behavior of others.*

When one has more power than someone else in a situation, like the power to affect one's playing time, scholarship, and status as a student, then one must accept the particular kinds of responsibility and care that come with that kind of power. There are appropriate ways to use that power and life-giving ways to compel certain kinds of behavior. For instance, team rules help create clear expectations; coaches and administrators have the power to enforce those rules for the good of the team and of the players themselves. Enforcement of these rules is an appropriate use of power. *When the power to compel certain behavior crosses the line into things that are matters of conscience like who to vote for in an election or where to stand on moral issues then one is misusing the power that he/she has to compel certain behavior.*

Religious belief and spirituality fall into this category of matters of the conscience. This protection of our personal capacity to believe what we choose to believe in matters of religion is the whence of our country's separation of church and state. Religious belief is not something the state should use its power to compel in its citizens.[8] The prevention of this kind of spiritual tyranny is something the American founders held as a high priority. The value of this integrity of the conscience is why state institutions are required by law not to endorse a particular religion. It is lawful for state institutions to be involved in conversations about religion and the study of

---

8. If you are dubious about the moral necessity of legally preventing the state from dictating our religious beliefs, think about if the state were promoting a faith other than your own. Would you feel the same way about the morality of the state using its power to compel you to accept the tenets of a faith other than your own?

religion as long as they are not endorsing one religion or using their power to compel people to adopt certain religious beliefs.

If a coach in a state funded university tells a player that he would be playing better if he would accept Jesus as his Savior, that is an abuse of power. If someone addresses the team at a mandatory meeting at a state university and tells them the team will win more games if they all follow Jesus, that is an abuse of power. When someone abuses power to pressure people about their faith everyone is diminished. What integrity does the decision to believe in God have for the one who assents because he or she is told to?

> *Everyone has power: it is the ability to have an impact, to act in a way that produces an effect.*
>
> *Some have more power than others because of the authority vested in a position they hold.*

Such abuses of power are also an affront to the remarkable ways that God works in and through each of us. It is a supreme act of trust to believe that all God is asking us to do is to witness to and testify about our faith to others; God is not asking us to make them believe what we do. We share our story; the rest is God's work. Why does it seem sometimes like deeply religious people have the most trouble trusting that God is at work that way? God doesn't need us to force our religion on other people. We may be a blessing along to way to someone, but you and I are not the reason someone changes his/her heart. God is.

We have been a part of college staffs where the authority vested in the position of coach or administrator has been abused around religion. We have supported athletes who have felt alienated or penalized by having religious beliefs that are different than those being openly encouraged by other coaches. We have worked to create spaces where athletes are free to wonder about religious questions without fear of reprisal. These situations that seemed to us to blatantly cross the line at the time, pale in comparison to the culture in place on the football team at Clemson University. The way that Christianity and football commingle at Clemson helps make this apocalypse even more revealing.

Head Coach Dabo Swinney has helped to build a winning program during his tenure at Clemson. And he makes no secret of how important he feels cultivating Christian values on the team are to that success. He tells recruits from the very beginning, "I'm a Christian. If you have a problem with that, you don't have to be here."[9] Coach Swinney's commitment to his faith is not problematic in and of itself. There appear to be several at least rhetorical ways that he tries to signal to players that he does not use one's faith to determine things like playing time. "When we get out on the football field, it's not about if you're a Christian, it's about who's the best player."[10]

At the same time, Christianity permeates the team culture to such a degree at Clemson that they baptize players on the practice field sometimes. The director of player development and assistant athletic director, Jeff Davis, a former Clemson and NFL player, is a preacher who uses Christian lessons in his work with the players. His office is called "The House of Truth" and he helped start a church just off campus that many players frequent. Team chaplain James Trapp has an office in the football offices, not a common setup with chaplains who serve teams at state funded universities. He leads weekly workshops for players as well as offer pastoral care. Coach Swinney keeps a Bible on his desk and often quotes scripture to players. One former player put it this way: "If you're there, you're going to know Jesus, you're going to know verses in the Bible—it's weaved into the culture. There's a drawing in towards Christianity."[11]

The success of Clemson's program not just on the playing field but in the improvement in graduation rates for players makes it hard to question the culture Coach Swinney and others have helped to create. That's how big-time sports works. If you are winning, you are given

> *The divine invitation to enter apocalypse creates tension and possibility; all is not lost.*

latitude on lots of things. *But the apocalypse asks us to look beneath the comfortable measures for what success looks like.* The apocalypse asks questions that reveal the demons that like to hide behind things that look and sound good. When it comes to religion and big-time sports, the questions we need to ask have to do with power—how we orient ourselves to God's power and how we choose to use our own power.

Christians often mistake our call to witness for a call to compel others to believe what we believe. The difference between these two approaches can sometimes be subtle, especially when we fail to take into account questions of power. While Coach Swinney and his staff may believe that you

9. Wolverton, "With God on Our Side," 2.

10. Ibid.

11. Ibid., 10.

don't have to be a Christian to feel like a part of the team or even to succeed on the team, the very nature of the power dynamics and the context make the situation ripe for distortions. Clemson is a state university, which forms the first problematic layer of the Christian culture unapologetically cultivated in the football program. State run institutions have a responsibility under the law to take great care not to endorse any particular religion. I am not sure there is a way to look at the football program and come away with any other conclusion than that Christianity is being endorsed. This layer is obvious and on the surface. If the law is being flouted, this would not be the first time a person of faith chose not to observe a law that he/she felt was unjust or unduly limiting. This kind of resistance is well founded in American culture—it is called civil disobedience. One of John's fellow coaches even used the term civil disobedience to describe his decision to encourage players to be Christian at a state university.

Civil disobedience is a choice about how to use one's power in a situation in which a higher power is imposing a law that violates one's conscience. Take a moment to consider the moral trajectory of engaging in civil disobedience in this particular kind of situation. A person with authority in a state school chooses to engage in civil disobedience by endorsing Christianity in resistance to a law, a higher power, in order to act on his religious conscience. However, the act of civil disobedience itself means that this person then becomes the higher power endorsing a religion to those who have less power than he does. *In this context the act of civil disobedience is itself replicating the inappropriate use of power that it is resisting.* It is an important ethical consequence to consider. The apocalypse makes the contradiction clear.

In the context of a coach and a player there are obvious power differences. The coach has both formal and informal channels of power. When the power differentials are as multilayered as they are the in coach/player relationship, there is no way for the coach's opinions and practices not to make a potent impression on players. There are power differentials because of age, many times race and economic status, involvement in decision-making structures, access to other power sources (media, university administrators, etc.), and the capacity to make life-altering decisions and impose them on others. These power differentials themselves are not necessarily problematic, but they create conditions that are prone to abuse. Those with more power have to take great pains not to overstep their bounds because of the multiple ways they have at their disposal to impact the behavior of others.

It is a sacred trust to be a coach, to be a minister, to be a parent, to be a therapist—all situations with easy pathways to abuse that can be both subtle and devastating at the same time. In all of these situations the temptation to use our power to control others in ways that diminish their agency and their power is a constant threat. These kinds of situations require clear boundaries to help those with more power leave space for those with less power to exercise their freedom of conscience.

The line to walk in the midst of these boundaries is very thin, especially when it is part of your job to help people figure out who they are. For those who are entrusted with this kind of power, it is a difficult line to walk when those under your charge are in need of guidance and are looking to you for it. Creating space for freedom of conscience and spiritual idiosyncrasy does not mean you cannot be a powerful guide. It simply means you are always careful to respect the way God made us and the way God works. Let us not mistaken our limited role in the lives of others for the all-encompassing way that God uniquely permeates each human life.

If we dig a little deeper in the Clemson situation, we uncover power dynamics that should raise questions for all people of faith. These questions press on us no matter our opinions about the state's role in the establishment of religion or even about the importance of using sports as a platform

Demonic distortions show themselves when we make something that is limited and finite into that which is infinite, into everything.

for Christian evangelism. If we honor God's unique power to transform the hearts of human beings, then we are left with questions about what room God has to work in situations where spiritual conformity is strongly encouraged. If we think we have all the answers for how God works in people's lives, we have crossed into truly dangerous territory. The first red flag in the inventory of power that the apocalypse enables is the distorted ways we want to make our limited, finite knowledge about God equal to everything there is to know about God. We can have all the best intentions about spreading God's power to transform human lives, but have the opposite effect when our particular (and limited) way of understanding and experiencing God does not resonate with someone. In our exuberance to share what has worked for us we can create false assumptions that what worked for us works for everyone.

Christianity has never been a cookie-cutter faith—Jesus was utterly adaptable to different needs and situations. And the faith that has built itself in his name has continued to bear the marks of his immediacy to what different people need from him. Sometimes following him means giving people the grace they need to encounter him in the ways that connect to their experience. If we are so busy trying to move people to where we think they need to be spiritually, they might miss the life-changing moment when Jesus can meet them where they truly are. As a pastor I have walked along-side people many, many times who are trying to find their way back to a place where they can truly meet Jesus. And in the process, they have to shed the guilt, shame, and even anger they have about the ways they were forced to understand Christ in religious contexts where the idiosyncrasies of their spirituality were not tolerated.

There is too little tolerance in big-time sports for differences in faith experiences. There is too much tolerance for the ways faith is used to chide players and is enlisted to manufacture a façade of team unity. *Football teams aren't that different than churches or any other system made up of people. Insistence on spiritual conformity is going to lead to alienation, hurt, and resentment for some people.* There are ways to be faithful that let people have space for their own experience. God is that big.

KEY PLAYERS

If a player wants to score touchdowns for Jesus, that's his call. With all the ways big-time athletes can be almost deified in our culture I would rather see a player who acknowledges that there is a higher power at work in his life than one who makes it all about himself. That awareness about our own power and the limits therein can be life-giving whether you are a believer of a particular stripe or not, or even a believer at all. If God has anything at all to do with football, then the end zone is big enough for all our religious differences, even the ones we don't completely understand.

The distortion born out of the monopoly of evangelical parachurch movements in the world of sports is, at its core, the assumption and aspiration of spiritual conformity. While I do not share many of the ways organizations like the FCA and AIA interpret the Christian tradition, these spaces of theological dissonance are not where the apocalypse unveils our most diminishing distortions. Just like these parachurch groups, other expressions of Christianity embody incomplete views of God and the Christian faith.

While such limitations should constantly give all of us pause as we walk the line of being believers and being human, the unveiling of our deepest distortion is not about our beliefs themselves.

The truth is that all stripes of Christians have failed to let Christianity in its most life-giving incarnations find a home in big-time sports. If it had, sports would not be so very conducive to the habits and patterns of white privilege, to the silencing of difference, to the hierarchies of gender, and to the pathologies of dishonesty, cheating, and violence.

Those who have power in the world of sports (e.g., university presidents, team owners, coaches, general managers, and athletic directors) who are practicing Christians but not closely aligned with groups like FCA sometimes seem to leave their Christianity at the church door. They avoid bringing their faith to bear on their work thus further authorizing the trivialization of Christianity and their community. This use of power is the shadow side of those who overstep their bounds by endorsing their faith. Those who extract out their faith in order to avoid endorsing it suffer from distortions that diminish Christianity just as much as enforced spiritual conformity does.

A similar hubris to those who say they have all the answers gives rise to the ways many Christians avoid any substantive spiritual or moral engagement with the world of sports. This theological stiff arm entails not only an immense lost opportunity for witnessing to the faith, but it also embodies a

> *. . . for I was hungry and you gave me no food, I was thirsty and you gave me nothing to drink, I was a stranger and you did not welcome me, naked and you did not give me clothing . . .*
> —*Matthew 25:42–43*

substantive moral failure. Why have so many Christians failed to engage such an iconic symbol of American culture with the prophetic voice that Christianity brings to all kinds of injustice? Why have all the different kinds of Christians who occupy the world of big-time sports failed to push back against things like racism, materialism, dishonesty, and violence?[12]

The Christian values that are not being shared in the world of big-time sports are the ones it needs the most. The aspects of the Christian faith that help us form transformative and beloved communities are actively

12. Krattenmaker and Hoffman pose questions about the inconsistency of only certain Christian values being held up in the sports world while others are seemingly ignored in situations where there are such glaring contradictions. Krattenmaker (*Onward Christian Athletes*, 196–201) raises the question in terms of racism, Hoffman (*Good Game*, 145–65) in terms of violence in games like football.

discouraged in big-time sports with the way power is used and abused on many levels. The NCAA manual is rife with regulations that prevent substantive relationships from forming and that discourage strong communities from being formed. Some of Jesus' clearest directives about how to be in beloved community have to do with responding to real human needs in our midst. But in Division I college football, when a player or his family is hungry, there are many situations in which we cannot give them food because it is an NCAA violation. If a player is cold and needs a coat, there are many barriers to giving him a coat, as it can constitute an improper benefit. In big-time sports people are treated as commodities with too much frequency—from coaches to players to everyone in between. Coaches and players are always on the edges of the communities they inhabit. Instead of being fully integrated members of the institutions and organizations they serve, they are forever haunted by just how expendable they are. No amount of money can compensate for the discouraging and repeated loss of community that players and coaches experience in this business. Racialized disadvantage is a statistically proven fact in big-time sports, and yet those called by God to be ambassadors of equity and love tolerate the inequities, and many of us benefit from them everyday. And former players with chronic illness caused by years of play, like dementia, have been left to largely fend for themselves financially and otherwise.

The apocalypse reveals the void that Christians have left in the world of big-time sports. Far from taking up too much space, Christianity has not taken up enough. Power is the muscle group we need to stretch and work in new ways. Sharing it, not abusing it, and making room for God to make the most of it, are the practices that call to us if we are serious about our yearning for a better world. Touchdowns for Jesus are fine by me as long as those of us who follow him are letting Jesus call the plays.

8

Redemption Time

Redemption is fundamentally about power. It is the power that begins to unbind every form of bondage and to unblock everything that resists the flow of the Divine Eros through creation.[1]

WHY DO SPORTS HAVE such a hold on us? And why should we care? *We began this unveiling of big-time sports with a simple idea: that our passion for sports springs from a deep desire in each of us for redemption.* We yearn for things to be as we hope they will be. Sports give us a place and a space to practice this yearning and to play with who we are and who we can become in the midst of our hopes and dreams. Even though this idea is simple, it embodies a profound complexity and it is veiled by many layers of illusion. This complexity and these illusions come from how we are made as human beings—we are absolutely dependent on God *and* we are prone to demonic distortions.

So we set our intention to search for God's fingerprints in the world of big-time sports with an eye toward what we can learn about ourselves and about God's healing invitation. Because of our tendency toward demonic distortions—toward mistaking what is finite for

> *Looking for signs of apocalypse is a quest for truth—truth that can be a signpost for what God is really looking for from human beings.*

---

1. Farley, *Wounding and Healing of Desire*, 28.

what is infinite, toward collapsing the universe into ourselves, and toward confusing our power with God's—we searched for these fingerprints by way of exorcising the demons that are so often exercised in big-time sports.

Because redemption is our goal, we want to learn from these demons, we want to know the truth. We desire the kind of truth that can set us free from the bondage of our distortions, the kind of truth that can help us understand the redemptive capacity of big-time sports. This is the kind of truth that can come from the power of apocalypse. *Apocalypse unveils, it reveals distortion, and it opens up space for transformation.*

Because a yearning for redemption drives us, we do not proceed in fear, but in faith. We trust that God's apocalypse calls us into our most deeply rooted distortions with healing in mind. In this book we have called out the hardest of our demons to name and claim: fanaticism, sexism, racism, privilege,

> *Apocalypse points us in the direction of instruction more than destruction.*

and abuse of power. And together we have worked to create the conditions necessary for us to harvest the fruits of apocalypse. It is these fruits that can nourish a new creation, new communities, and new ways of being in the world that are life-giving for us all.

WALK THROUGH

A walk back through what we have witnessed with the lifted veil in big-time sports reminds us of all the ground we have covered. With each piece of the veil lifted, we have been offered new frameworks for understanding our passion for big-time sports and ourselves. And with each new framework we have had to practice new ways of seeing things, new ways of uncovering our distortions. And with these new eyes to see, we have also caught glimpses of the redemptive capacity inherent in sports.

"Encountering the Fan(tasm)": The fan(tasm) holds a mirror up to us about ourselves, not simply revealing human falleness but surfacing our deep yearning for redemption. We gazed at the stadium as not a trivial place, but as a space where we play with our own power, with our profound longing for things to be as we hope they will be. The fan(tasm) embodies this play and this longing in a mode that both suspends and reveals reality. The apocalypse reveals the opportunity to see our own desires in a new light. If the spectacle of the fan(tasm) is allowed to take up space as a figment of our redemptive desire then we can more clearly practice and play with what redemption could really be in the larger world. When we let this play cultivate our dependence on God, then this play can be revitalizing and regenerating. If we are blind to the true source of these deep longings, then we collapse our play into trivializing distortions. We kid ourselves into thinking that our desire is really just about the team or the game. And we diminish the redemptive capacity that sports have. The fan(tasm) creates opportunity even as it plays with fire.

"Man Up": We explored the constrained spaces of gender performance that big-time sports often have on display. And we wondered together how much sports like football depend on gendered caricatures and stereotypes. The apocalypse revealed the ways these constrained spaces diminish the lives not just of women, but also of men. We exorcised the demon of our collective fear of ambiguity. We also allowed ourselves to wonder if these constrained spaces for gender performance could be contributing to some of the diminished popularity of football. More generous space for people to find their way in the world of football as they are could change everything from the prevalence of concussions to the barriers that keep women from the game. From this generous space we are better equipped to hear and to respond to the most difficult challenges our communities face. Maybe there is more to football than the constrained spaces that it often occupies.

"White Lines": We surfaced some of the oftentimes hard to notice boundaries and barriers created by white privilege and internalized racism in big-time sports. We shifted our frame of reference for how sports and race intersect. Instead of focusing on civil rights iconography, we allowed sports to hold up a mirror to us. Reflected back are some of our most tenacious and unconscious habits of mind. The apocalypse reveals disadvantage where American culture has told us there is advantage. The apocalypse reveals white obliviousness where we have labeled things as "normal." We began dismantling the scaffolding of these distortions and we set our gaze on the spaces of disadvantage that exist for young men of color in big-time sports. The white lines displayed their capacity to diminish relationships and communities, especially in those spaces where we need stronger connections and understanding for things to move in a more life-giving direction. Lifting the veil on the white lines gives us a chance to (e)race them by seeing them more clearly. Only then can we build the relationships and communities we need to make them disappear.

"Higher Learning": Sometimes higher learning takes going back to the basics. The apocalypse when it comes to big-time sports on university campuses reveals some deeply seated distortions. The crisis of integrity revealed, however, is not where it has been placed for decades in the "athletics versus academics" debate. Far from simply defining the problem, these distortions have set the tone around how to address a complex set of issues that arise when big-time sports and academia cohabitate. The unveiling gave us a new framework for understanding how learning communities are diminished when athletes' academic success is measured by eligibility. And we learned how the ways power is often used cuts off healthy circulation in communities that want to understand themselves as place of growth and learning for diverse groups. The white lines of privilege surfaced again in clear relief. And we were able to see how power dynamics and white obliviousness have diminished relationships and fractured communities.

"Touchdowns for Jesus": Christianity and big-time sports can appear to have a very cozy relationship. The apocalypse shows us a more complicated story. We found the marks of trivialized faith, abuse of power, and demonic distortions that kid us into thinking we know everything there is to know about who God is and how God works. Both the expressions of Christianity that have found a home in big-time sports and the expressions of Christianity that have kept big-time sports at arms' length have failed to interrogate power—God's power and ours. The unveiling laid bare the distortions of power that have diminished relationships the most.

REDEMPTION TIME PLAYBOOK

The question now is how we focus these new frameworks, these new eyes to see, on cultivating new practices of redemption. The next step in our unveiling is a decision: will we respond to the offer God extends to us out of apocalypse—the invitation to be transformed? Can we recommit ourselves in the world of big-time sports to honoring the greatest gifts that sports have to offer to us: the gifts of vitality, of community, and of transformation? These gifts embody the redemptive capacity of sports. The challenge is how to reclaim these gifts and practice them as we unbind ourselves from our distortions. We need practices that transform our distortion—formations in our collective playbook that can habituate new, more life-giving ways of being in the world for all of us. These practices can inform the ways we build relationships, the way we form communities, and the way we understand a greater purpose in our lives. These formations are built through the habituation of pulse-taking, relationship-making, and groundbreaking.

For these formations to be transforming they require practice, practice, practice.

Formation #1: Pulse-Taking

My college cross-country coach, Dick Burchett, use to take us by cemeteries on our long runs. He would point toward the gravestones and say, "It is good to remember that no matter how slow you are going, you are going faster than they are." It was a vivid reminder of the gift of vitality inherent in sports. Simple movement is part of what is

> *Pulse-taking seeks out the ways sports better acquaint us with feeling alive.*

beautiful about sports. And this movement and breath help us remember our vitality. Coach Burchett gave us a way to allow vitality to be a measure for our well-being as athletes, apart from speed or time or finish in a race. John has always said that good teams don't talk about winning; they talk about having a good practice today. They focus on the now, they focus on the process. John and I often give thanks for the ways sports call us back to the now in ways that increase our vitality. They keep us grounded in step-by-step moments. They kindle a trust in us that attending to the step-by-step will allow good things to unfold.

We catch glimpses of the capacity of sports to cultivate vitality. Pulse-taking acknowledges our need to practice redemption, to practice disappointment, to play with our power to have an impact. Pulse-taking is the art of trying on for size the intuitions, desires, and outcomes of how redemp-

> *Pulse-taking practices redemption by making vitality a measure of our well-being.*

tion works in human life. Giving the most life-giving framework to our collective obsession with sports allows it to be a regenerating, clarifying practice instead of a bewildering and diminishing stirring up of toxic emotions. Our passion is not just about the team, it's about us, about how we are made, and about what we can become.

The practice of pulse-taking involves regularly checking in with ourselves to make sure we understand the source of our desires and the object of our yearning. Pulse-taking makes space for a deeper, more profound framework for our passion than we often are given in big-time sports. Pulse-taking is not afraid of more generous spaces for play and for performance, spaces that make room for ambiguity. *The practice of pulse-taking slowly transforms ambiguity from something to be feared into something that multiplies vitality and zest.* We learn how to trust the complexity of life and of each other in ways that are expansive, not diminishing. The capacity of sports to regenerate our bodies, our communities, even our souls, is allowed to take center stage.

Formation #2: Relationship-Making

John and I were newly married when I went to a baby shower hosted by one of the other Carolina Panthers' coaches' wives. We were a brand new staff so some of our conversation at the shower was just about getting to know each other. One of the wives asked how long we had been married and if we had kids yet. When I answered her question with and

> *Relationship-making puts energy into building strong, lasting connections with others.*

"about six weeks" and "no" she laughed and shook her head. She then told a story to fill me in on the world I had just entered. "I remember when my oldest son was about three or four years old," she said. "It was Valentine's Day or my birthday or something. The doorbell rang and my son ran to the door and opened it to find a florist with a delivery for me. He asked who the flowers were from and the florist looked at the card and told my son, 'They are from Joe.' [Her husband's name is Joe.] And my son looked at me with a curious look on his face and said, 'Whatever happened to Joe?'"

The room full of football coaches' wives erupted in laughter. I laughed, too, but felt a sense of foreboding at the same time. The idea of a child not even remembering who his dad is because he was at work all the time was troubling to me. Lots of wives use to joke that NFL stands for "No Family Life." And in many ways they are right. I use to think that the NFL was anti-family, but the longer I am around big-time football, the clearer I am on a different conclusion. It is not the family in particular that big-time football conspires against; all relationships have been diminished by some of football's most prevalent patterns and practices.

One of the clearest patterns that has diminished all relationships in big-time football is that people are commodities. And commodities don't build strong communities. They build capital and profit, but not mutuality, loyalty, and life-giving relationships. The redemptive practice of relationship-making pushes back against this commodification. Relationship-making finds ways to value people for what they bring to the community over the long haul. Relationship-making puts a premium on the inherent value of people by resisting the habits of using them and discarding them when they are no longer profitable to have around.

There are several easy ways to practice relationship-making when redemption is our goal. Sharing power, facilitating access to decision-making, creating generous space for diversity, committing to mechanisms for long-term commitment and care, and developing rewards for loyalty over time are just a few. Investing in

> *Relationship-making values people as an end in themselves, not as a means to an end.*

people over the long haul is against the grain in big-time football. But, as far as big-time sports goes, football is ripe to practice relationship-making in ways that could make a huge impact. This symphony of sports lends itself to a powerful kind of investment in people. Football, at its core, is about a diverse group of people with different skills coming together to make things happen in ways that others do not anticipate. Just think how much more life-giving big-time sports could be if conditions were conducive to building healthy communities of people who were valued and honored for who they are over time. If we could build trust with each other, share our gifts, have equitable and just systems of reward and merit, and have transparent and consistent systems of justice and fairness, we might build communities, organizations, and institutions that exceed anything we've imagined.

One of the greatest gifts of sports comes from the life lessons of being on a team. We learn to carry each other's burdens. We learn to do our part for something greater than our own self-interest. We connect with others in ways we can't in other contexts. Sports can bring people together across class, race, and life circumstance. And these lessons and opportunities have been overpowered by rules and regulations, by the messages that tell people they are free agents and they are on their own. Once we forget our interdependence and begin to neglect the ties that bind, things will unravel from there. Trust erodes, families fracture, friendships atrophy, power becomes concentrated, resources are hoarded, and the rulebooks get bigger and bigger and bigger.

Relationship-making practices basic steps that create communities that are strong and that have staying power. Systems built on an "every man for himself" mentality are built on lies about our very created nature. And none of us deserves to be treated as if we are alone in the world. Because, at the very core of who we are and how we are made, we are not free agents.

We need each other for life-giving community to emerge. Only then can the distortions that diminish our connections give way to the change we need—so that everyone who contributes to the world of big-time sports can thrive.

Formation #3: Groundbreaking

Working to get better is a way of life in sports. That drive and determination can yield life-changing results. When that same drive and determination becomes distorted it is being fueled by a haunting insecurity—the burden of

> *The practice of ground-breaking is about leaving a place better than you found it.*

what you are not. When John was named the offensive coordinator for the Chicago Bears he became one of the youngest people ever to call a game in the NFL. It was an exciting time, and it was also a challenging time.

When superlatives are swirling around you that say you're the best thing since sliced bread, the laws of physics tell us you could be headed for a fall. Those hyped up statements will be balanced at some point by equally extreme negativity. What goes up must come down. In a business as volatile as football, you have to be intentional about grounding yourself in something more substantial than these fickle sources of praise and blame. And the drive to break new ground, to be the first, to be the youngest, to be the best needs a richer reservoir to draw from than individual success for it to really make the world a better place. The truth is that coaches often do some of their best work during the seasons when their records are the worst. Much of the work they do is invisible and often not valued. Far from rewarding the grit, leadership, and vision that many coaches use to help teams weather difficult times, these herculean efforts are answered with the ritual annual firings. The "coaching carousel" is a source of media interest and Internet chatter like no other. And it is fed by the distortions that make us think being good at something and being a valuable part of a community is the same as winning all the time. The redemptive practice of groundbreaking is not grounded in superlatives or in hype, it is kindled in us by our Creator, the one who made us to be innovative, creative, and persistent beings.

The practice of groundbreaking is not fueled by insecurity. Far from it, it is fueled by love—love of sports, love of team, love of the game, love of life, and love of God. Christianity is all about breaking new ground—that is what Jesus did and that is what he asks us to do—to break through social boundaries, to question hallowed ways of doing things, to leave the world better than how it was when we came into it. And we do these things because of love.

THE BIG GAME

If you are tangled up in the world of big-time sports, somewhere within you is a love of sports. You are, on some level, passionate about the fact that sports matter. If you have forgotten that love, if you have neglected it, think back to when that love was what motivated you and what made you hungry for more. It is that love that must kindle in us a resolve to face the demons that conspire to harm the sports we love, to diminish them, and in some cases even to destroy them. We love these games we play because they help us connect to others, they help us feel alive, and they help us embody gratitude for the gifts God has given us. And these games we play give us a space to play with who we are, who we hope we can be, and who God is calling us to become.

Sports embody our deep yearning for redemption—that the world can be a place where fair play wins and hard work pays off and entrusting ourselves to a life-giving cause makes the world a better place. We long for a world where things work the way they are supposed to, where we understand who we are in the scheme of things, and where we feel the connections and possibilities we need to thrive. We play with these desires and we practice what it takes to endure what life actually hands us. Sports increase your creativity, your clarity of mind, your ability to work through problems, your ability to control anger, and your ability to endure difficult times. These are much more than the games we play. It is here that we can practice becoming better at being who we were created to be in the first place.

If there is one thing we know how to do in sports, it is practice. When it comes to redemption, we need to practice and practice more. We might be amazed by what we can become when we habituate fearless wisdom with a work ethic that won't quit and a cast of millions of people who care with a passion that seems unbound. If the world of big-time sports sets its mind to playing with society's most tenacious problems with healing in mind, you better believe things can change for the better. It sounds religious, cosmic, even mysteriously divine.

Afterword

BEFORE MARCIA DELIVERS A sermon, posts a blog, publishes a poem, or writes a chapter, I get to read or hear it before anyone else. Her writing stimulates conversations ranging from theology, ethics, fairness, and justice to parenting, team morale, motivation, and even play calling. Our talks are sometimes intense and we don't always come out at the same place. Marcia regularly asks me to look at topics through lenses I had never considered or even knew existed. In the twenty-four years I have known Marcia she has always stretched my mind, heart, and soul in ways that make me a better person. And her pushing, prodding, and pulling are always towards justice and fairness.

I was nervous when Marcia started writing her "Calling Audibles" blog series. It felt like our intimate conversations about what was happening in our lives was out there for public consumption. And in many ways, they were. With each blog post Marcia invited more people into the conversation. And with each blog post, more people added their voice. And the conversation became very rich; we both learned and grew from it in ways that made us better people. In *Touchdowns for Jesus and Other Signs of the Apocalypse* Marcia extends the same invitation to anybody and everybody with an interest in and connection to big-time sports. The invitation is to a deep conversation about why big-time sports have such a strong hold on American culture and why we should care.

Together, Marcia and I have lived each chapter in this book. We realize there are big and difficult questions facing sports at every level. This book talks to the vociferous, face-painted fan who thinks the play calling stinks. This book stands up for the young woman athlete who wears hand-me-down uniforms from the mens' team. And it names the objectification of women in big-time sports for what it is, sexism. As a man, I find this chapter ("Man Up") discomforting. But, as I tell players I coach, if you're not willing to leave your comfort zone you will never grow, you will never get better. This chapter speaks also to men about how the same barriers that have harmed women in sports diminish the lives of men, too. Marcia calls white men of privilege and the young athletes upon whose labor millions of dollars are made to come to the table together. This book hopes that academicians will begin to take the lead and meet young men and women where they are in their educational journeys. And she calls on all people of faith to be generous and kind and to create space for God to do God's work. In this conversation, all voices are valued.

I believe good morale is the most important ingredient on a winning football team. If good morale develops on a team, it is because everyone on the team fosters it. It is not accidental. Developing good morale on a football team is a difficult task. The diversity that exists on a team is one of football's greatest resources. At the same time, bringing people from every walk of life together into the same meeting room and locker room is not without its challenges. Morale is especially delicate on big-time football teams because it is the only sport in the world where the same players don't play offense and defense. On teams where morale is not intentionally tended to these dynamics can create divisions that can kill a team. The great thing about football is that it is a place where team needs always supersede individual wants. And so these dynamics can be channeled into forming a community of people who do things no one expected they could do.

As our culture has become more individualistic so has the game of football. In 2001, I remember being confronted by a fan for handing the ball to Anthony Thomas in the red zone too much when I called the plays for the Chicago Bears. This individual had our star wide receiver, Marty Booker, on his fantasy football team and wanted him to score. Never mind that our team was 13–3 with the best record since the 1985 Chicago Bears Super Bowl team. On another occasion, I worked with a coach who once told me, "If we can just lead the league in passing, we'll all get better jobs." While that team threw for lots of yards, our record was 4–12 and we constantly put our defense in terrible situations. It has never been harder to put the collective good ahead of individual honors and gain. And that is exactly what Marcia is asking us to do. This book is a chance to foster good morale in big-time sports for all who give them so much. It is a chance to be intentional about how we work together to become better.

In the chapter on gender, Marcia writes, "Apocalypse tells us that what we stand to lose when we don't ask the difficult questions is actually the more radical threat to our humanity that the erosion of the social convention in question is." If we don't address problems in big-time sports we risk losing to them. I pray this book brings people together into the conversations necessary to preserve all that is good about sports. I pray that whoever reads this book and enters into the conversation is pushed, prodded, and pulled towards what is fair and just.

—John Mount Shoop
West Lafayette, Indiana

Bibliography

Ashburn, Elyse. "At Elite Colleges, Legacy Status May Count More than Was Previously Thought." *The Chronicle of Higher Education*, January 5, 2011. http://chronicle.com/article/Legacys-Advantage-May-Be/125812/.

Barra, Allen. "America's Most Dangerous Football Is in the Pee Wee Leagues, Not the NFL." *The Atlantic*, August 31, 2013. http://www.theatlantic.com/entertainment/archive/2013/08/americas-most-dangerous-football-is-in-the-pee-wee-leagues-not-the-nfl/279229/.

Bonilla-Silva, Eduardo. *Racism without Racists: Color-Blind Racism and Racial Inequality in Contemporary America*. 3rd ed. Lanham, MD: Rowman and Littlefield, 2010.

Branch, Taylor. "The Shame of College Sports." *The Atlantic*, September 7, 2011. http://www.theatlantic.com/magazine/archive/2011/10/the-shame-of-college-sports/308643/2/.

Carter, Andrew. "UNC's Thorp Calls NCAA Sanctions 'Painful.'" *Raleigh News & Observer*, March 13, 2012. http://www.newsobserver.com/2012/03/13/1926741/ncaa-to-announce-findings-on-unc.html.

"Connecting the Dots." *The Daily Tar Heel*, September 22, 2010. http://www.dailytarheel.com/article/2010/09/connecting_the_dots.

Crawley, A. Bruce. "122 Teams, One Black Major Owner." *The Philadelphia Tribune*, October 23, 2011. http://www.phillytrib.com/commentaryarticles/item/1164–122-teams-one-black-major-owner.html.

Curliss, J. Andrew. "Thorp: UNC's Standards for Athletes Will Rise." *Raleigh News & Observer*, September 26, 2012. http://www.newsobserver.com/2012/09/26/2371972/thorp-uncs-standards-for-athletes.html.

Deace, Steve. "Don't Ruin the Game We Love." *USA Today*, January 30, 2013. http://www.usatoday.com/story/opinion/2013/01/30/football-super-bowl-steve-deace/1879063/.

Dulac, Gerry. "Uneasy Lies the Head that Wears the Headset." *Pittsburgh Post-Gazette*, January 29, 2012. http://www.post-gazette.com/sports/steelers/2012/01/29/Uneasy-lies-the-head-that-wears-the-headset/stories/201201290158.

Farley, Wendy. *Tragic Vision and Divine Compassion: A Contemporary Theodicy*. Louisville: Westminster John Knox, 1990.

———. *The Wounding and Healing of Desire: Weaving Heaven and Earth*. Louisville: Westminster John Knox, 2005.

Foucault, Michel. "Theatrum Philosophicum." In *Language, Counter-memory, Practice: Selected Essays and Interviews*, edited by Donald F. Bouchard, translated by Donald F. Bouchard and Sherry Simon, 165–96. Ithaca, NY: Cornell University Press, 1977.

Friedlander, Brett. "UNC Decides to Lawyer Up, Baddour Explains the Silence." *Wilmington Star-News*, August 14, 2010. http://acc.blogs.starnewsonline.com/14912/unc-decides-to-lawyer-up-baddour-explains-the-silence/.

Frilingos, Christopher. *Spectacles of Empire: Monsters, Martyrs, and the Book of Revelation.* Philadelphia: University of Pennsylvania Press, 2004.

Ganim, Sara. "UNC Whistle-Blower Battles for OK to Study Student-Athlete Literacy." *CNN.com*, January 17, 2014. http://www.cnn.com/2014/01/17/us/ncaa-athletes-unc-investigation/.

Gillespie, Michael. "Players and Spectators: Sports and Ethical Training in the American University." In *Debating Moral Education: Rethinking the Role of the Modern University*, edited by Elizabeth Kiss, et al., 296–316. Durham, NC: Duke University Press, 2010.

Hall, Erika V., and Robert Livingston. "The Hubris Penalty: Biased Responses to 'Celebration' Displays of Black Football Players." *Journal of Experimental Social Psychology* 48 (2012) 899–904.

Harper, Shaun R., and Stephen John Quaye, eds. *Student Engagement in Higher Education: Theoretical Perspectives and Practical Approaches to Diverse Populations.* New York: Routledge, 2009.

Harper, Shaun R., Collin D. Williams Jr., and Horatio W. Blackman. "Black Male Student-Athletes and Racial Inequities in NCAA Division I College Sports." Philadelphia: University of Pennsylvania, Center for the Study of Race and Equity in Education, 2013. www.gse.upenn.edu/equity/sports.

Higher Education Center for Alcohol and Other Drug Abuse and Violence Prevention. "Fraternity and Sorority Members and Alcohol and Other Drug Abuse." August 2008. http://files.eric.ed.gov/fulltext/ED537622.pdf.

Hoffman, Shirl James. *Good Game: Christianity and the Culture of Sports.* Waco, TX: Baylor University Press, 2010.

Knight Commission on Intercollegiate Athletics. *A Call to Action: Reconnecting College Sports and Higher Education.* 2001. http://www.knightcommission.org/images/pdfs/2001_knight_report.pdf.

———. *Keeping Faith with the Student Athlete: A New Model for Intercollegiate Athletics.* 1991. http://www.knightcommission.org/images/pdfs/1991–93_kcia_report.pdf.

———. *Restoring the Balance: Dollars, Values, and the Future of College Sports.* 2010. http://www.knightcommission.org/restoringthebalance.

Krattenmaker, Tom. *Onward Christian Athletes: Turning Ballparks into Pulpits and Players into Preachers.* Lanham, MD: Rowman and Littlefield, 2010.

Lavigne, Paula. "Concussion News Worries Parents: OTL Survey Finds 57 Percent of Parents Less Likely to Allow Kids to Play Football." *ESPN.com*, August 26, 2012. http://espn.go.com/espn/otl/story/_/id/8297366/espn-survey-finds-news-coverage-concussions-leads-majority-parents-less-likely-allow-sons-play-youth-football-leagues.

McIntosh, Peggy. *White Privilege and Male Privilege: A Personal Account of Coming to See Correspondences through Work in Women's Studies.* Wellesley College, Center for Research on Women, 1988. http://www.iub.edu/~tchsotl/part2/McIntosh%20White%20Privilege.pdf.

Mount Shoop, Marcia W. *Let the Bones Dance: Embodiment and the Body of Christ.* Louisville: Westminster John Knox, 2010.

Potupchuk, Maggie. "White Culture Handout." http://www.mpassociates.us/home.php.

Putney, Clifford. *Muscular Christianity: Manhood and Sports in Protestant America, 1880–1920.* Cambridge, MA: Harvard University Press, 2001.

Race—The Power of an Illusion. 2003. Californian Newsreel. http://newsreel.org/video/RACE-THE-POWER-OF-AN-ILLUSION and http://www.pbs.org/race/000_General/000_00-Home.htm.

Rail, Genevieve, and Jean Harvey. "Body at Work: Michel Foucault and the Sociology of Sport." *Sociology of Sport Journal* 12 (1995) 164–79.

Said, Edward. *Orientalism.* New York: Pantheon, 1978.

Schleiermacher, Friedrich. *The Christian Faith.* 2 vols. New York: Harper & Row, 1963.

Seward, Mickey. "60 Years and Counting." *FCA Magazine* 56.1 (2013). http://www.fca.org/themagazine/60-years-and-counting/#.Ux4SLPSwI-M.

Sölle, Dorothee. *Thinking about God: An Introduction to Theology.* Translated by John Bowden. Philadelphia: Trinity, 1990.

Shoop, John. "Thanks, Amazing Student Athletes." *Chapelboro.com*, November 22, 2012. http://chapelboro.com/huddle-up-2012/the-shoop-scoop/thanks-amazing-student-athletes/.

Southall, Richard. "Oral Remarks delivered to Rawlings Panel." 2013. University of North Carolina, Chapel Hill, NC. http://rawlingspanel.web.unc.edu/.

Staurowsky, Ellen, and Ramogi Huma. *The Price of Poverty in Bigtime College Sports.* National College Players Association. http://assets.usw.org/ncpa/The-Price-of-Poverty-in-Big-Time-College-Sport.pdf.

Steinfeldt, Jesse, et al. "Moral Atmosphere and Masculine Norms in American College Football." *The Sport Psychologist* 26 (2012) 341–58. https://scholarworks.iu.edu/dspace/bitstream/handle/2022/15244/2012%20steinfeldt.pdf?sequence=1.

Tillich, Paul. *Systematic Theology.* Vol. 2. Chicago: University of Chicago Press, 1957.

Vigen, Aana Marie. "To Hear and to Be Accountable across Difference: An Ethic of White Listening." *Disrupting White Supremacy from Within: White People on What We Need to Do,* edited by Jennifer Harvey, Karin A. Case, and Robin Hawley Gorsline, 216–48. Cleveland: Pilgrim, 2004.

Wise, Tim. *Colorblind: The Rise of Post-racial Politics and the Retreat from Racial Equity.* San Francisco: City Lights, 2010.

———. "Default Position: Reflections on the Brain-Rotting Properties of Privilege." In *Speaking Treason Fluently: Anti-racist Reflections from an Angry White Male.* Berkeley, CA: Soft Skull, 2008.

Wolverton, Brad. "With God on Our Side." *The Chronicle of Higher Education,* November 27, 2013. http://chronicle.com/article/With-God-on-Our-Side/143231/.

Young, Iris Marion. "Throwing Like a Girl." In *Body and Flesh: A Philosophical Reader,* edited by Donn Welton, 259–73. Malden, MA: Blackwell, 1998.

———. "Throwing Like a Girl Revisited." In *Body and Flesh: A Philosophical Reader,* edited by Donn Welton, 286–90. Malden, MA: Blackwell, 1998.

Made in the USA
Coppell, TX
13 January 2020